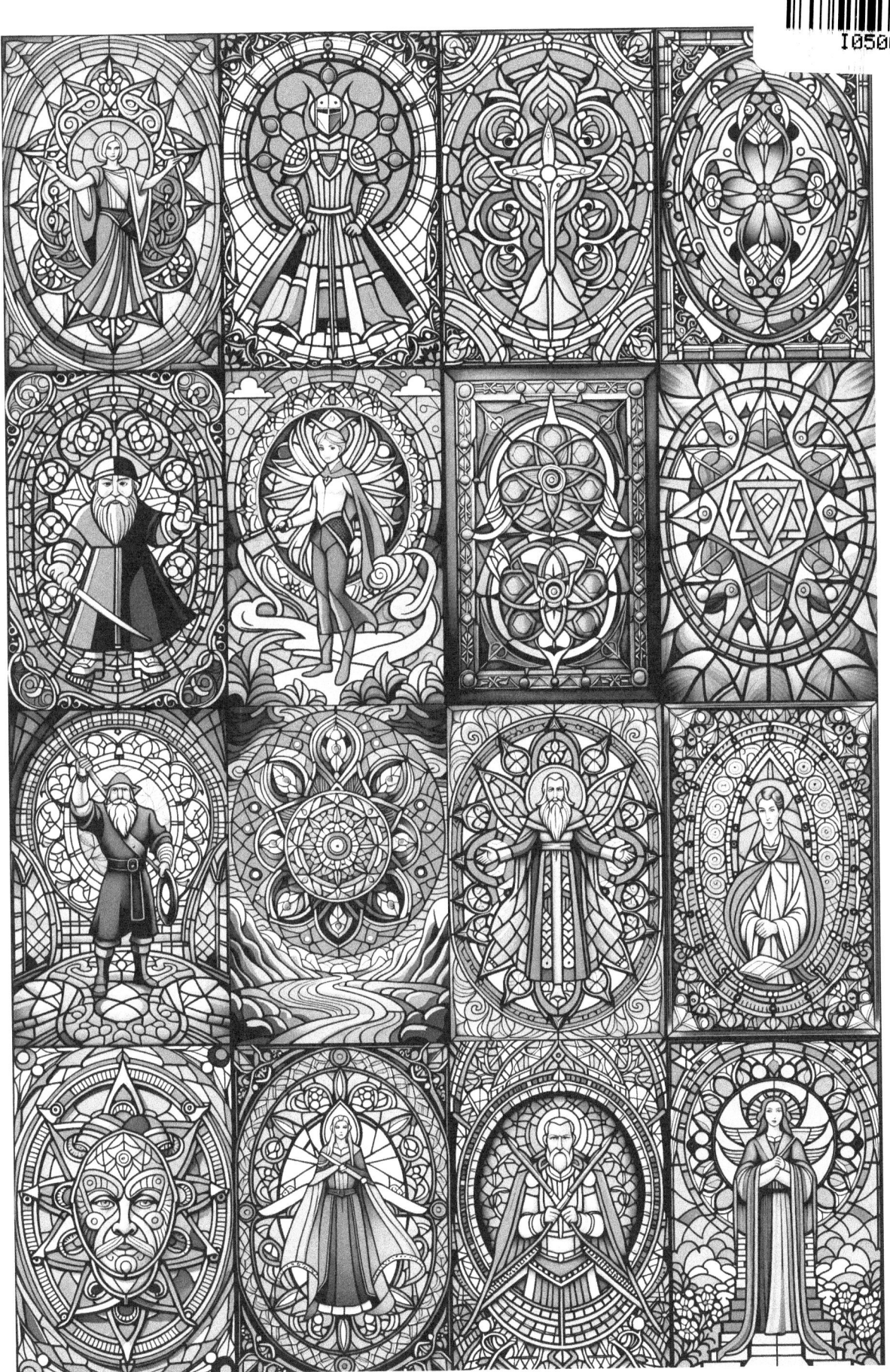

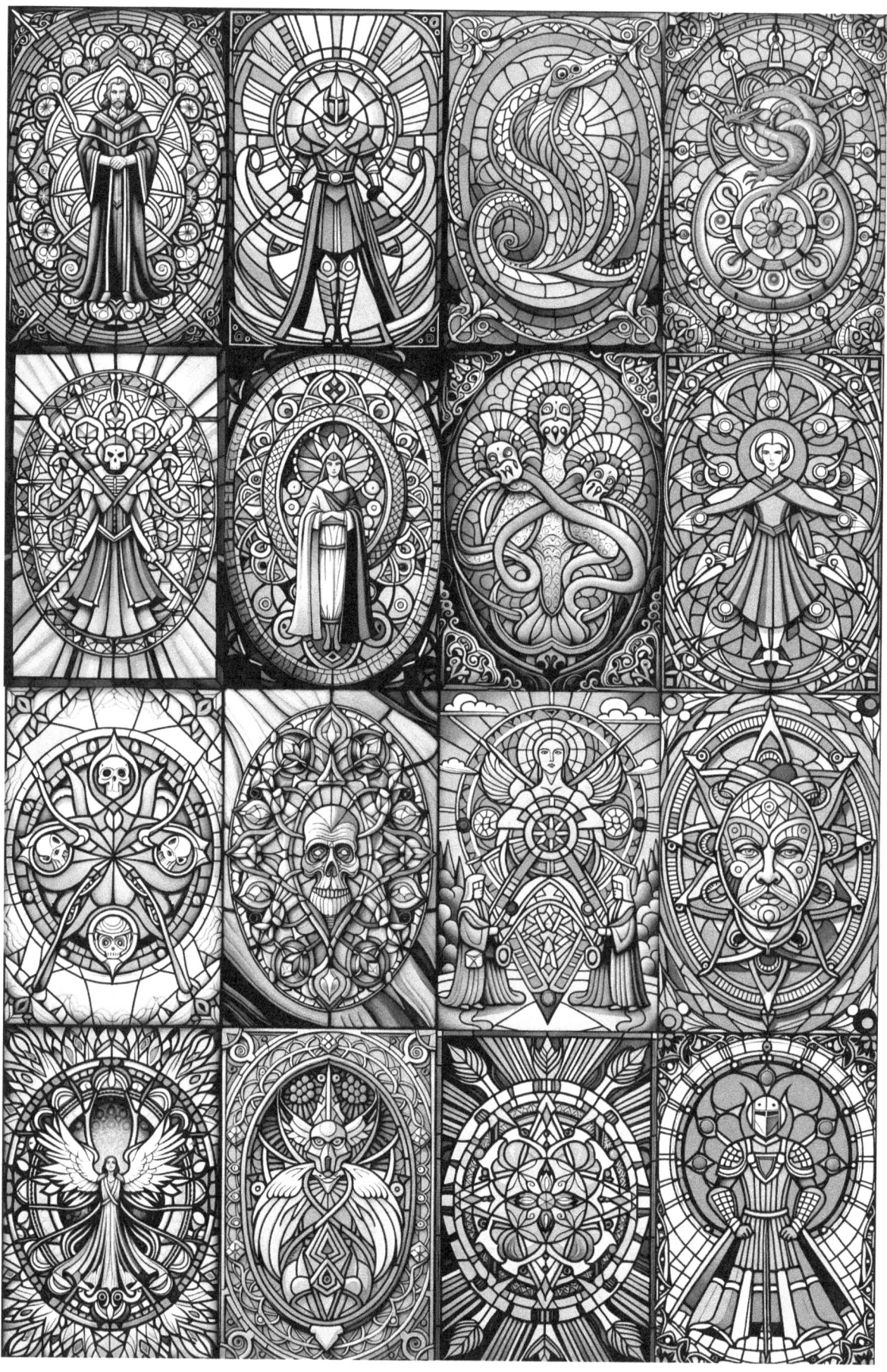

MEDIEVAL MANDALA

COLORING BOOK

BY CHROMATIC COLOR BOY

ACKNOWLEDGMENTS:

TO IRENE,
FOR ALWAYS SUPPORTING ME IN MY CRAZY IDEAS.

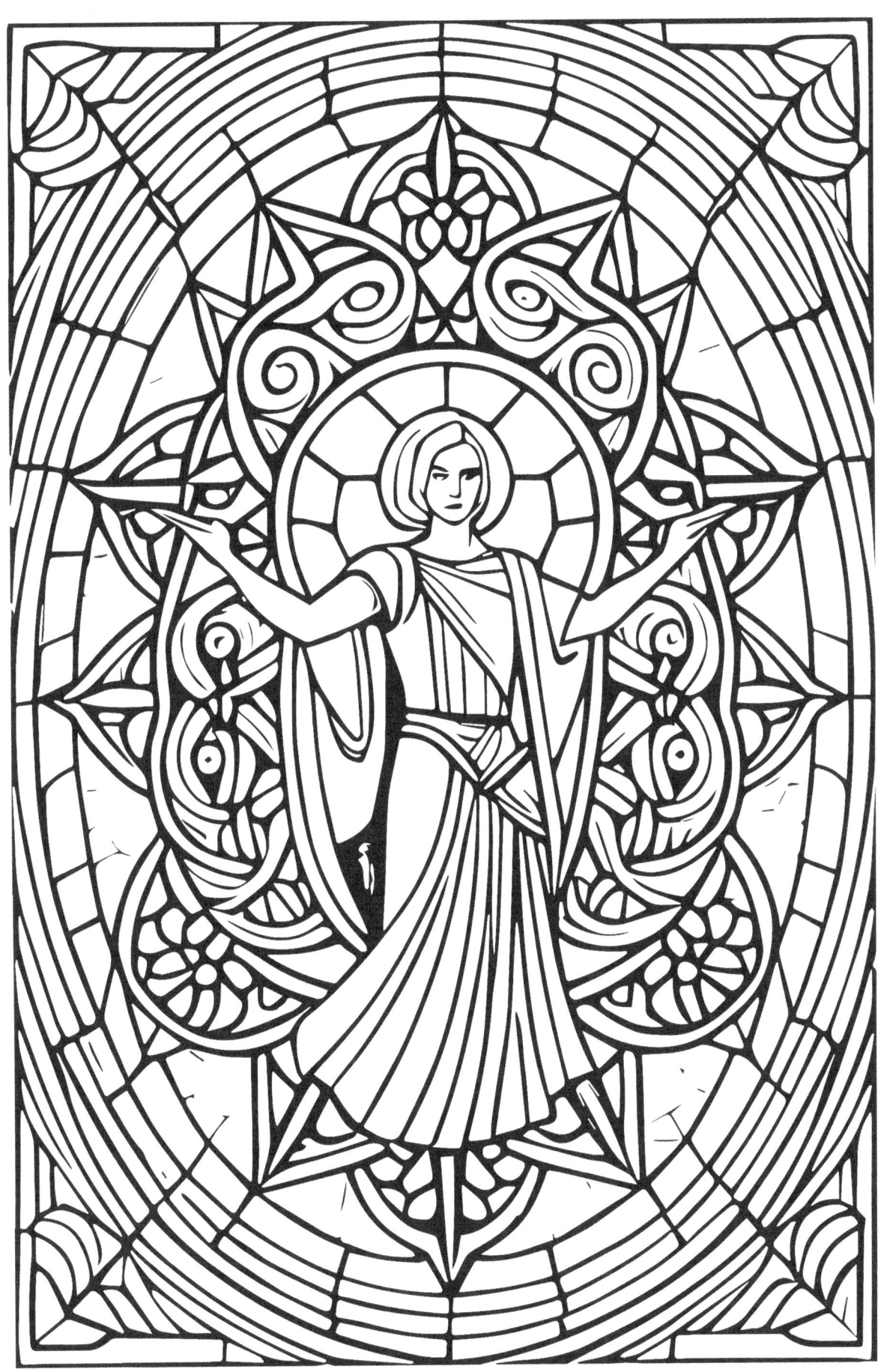

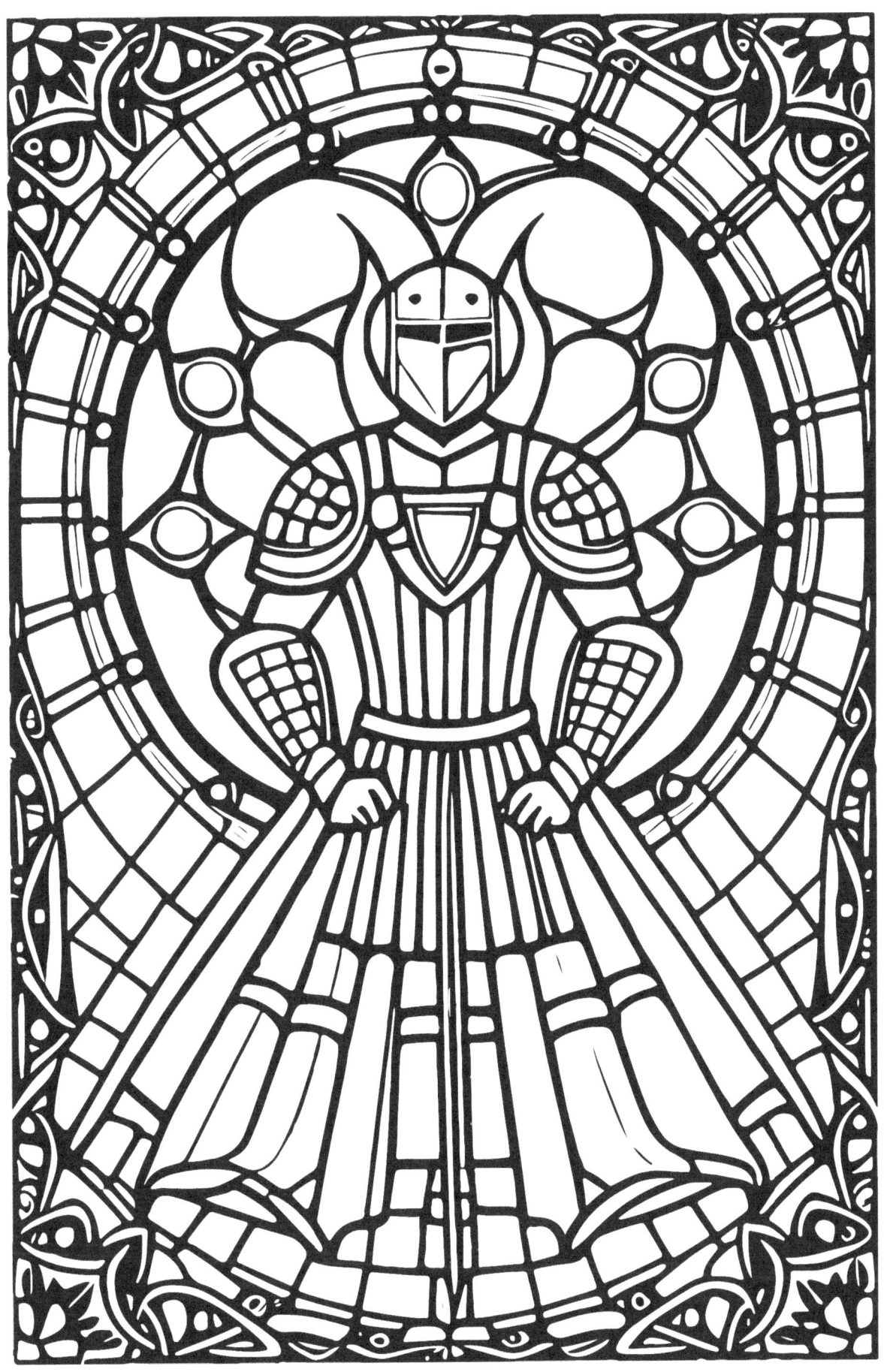

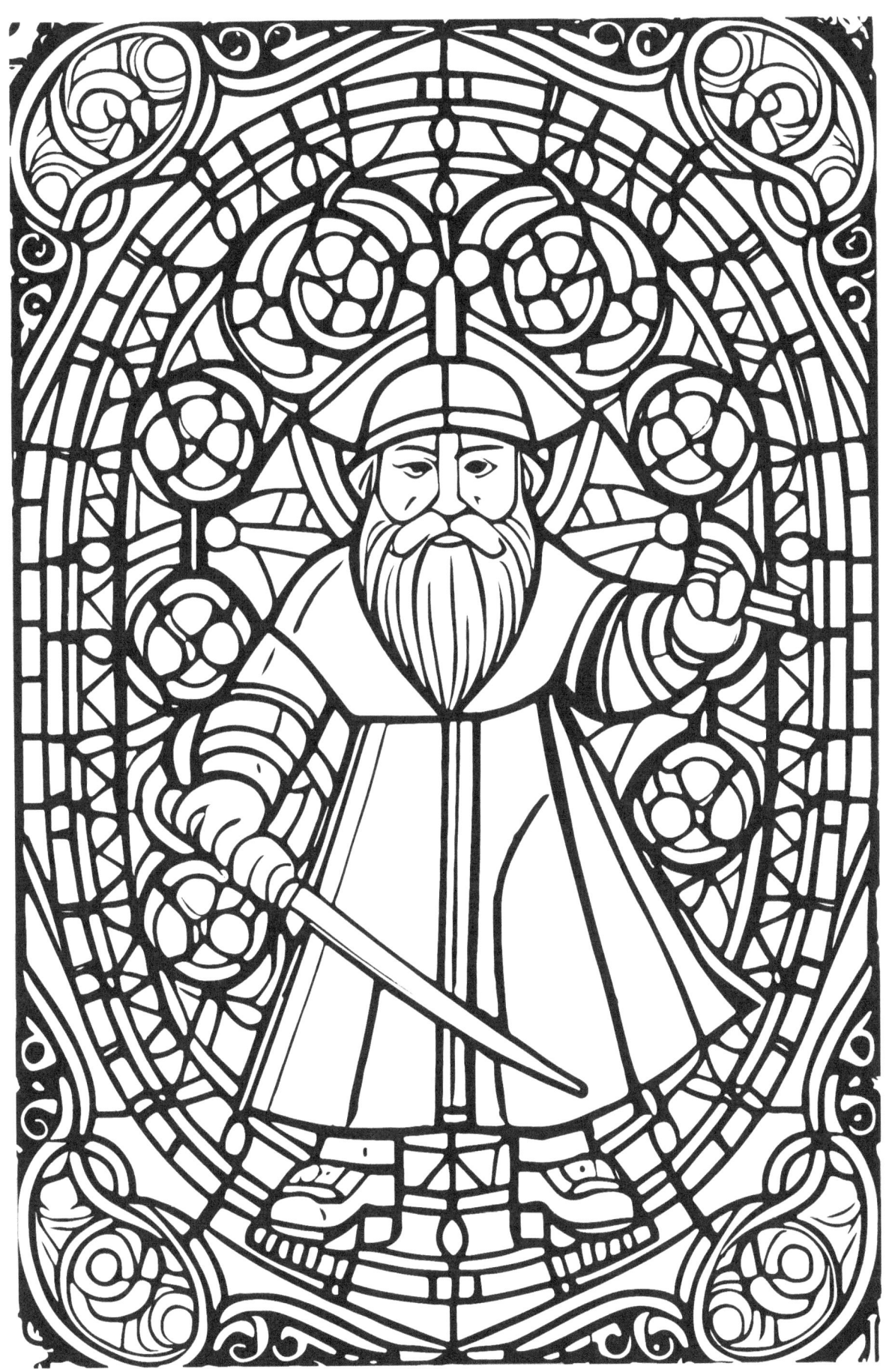

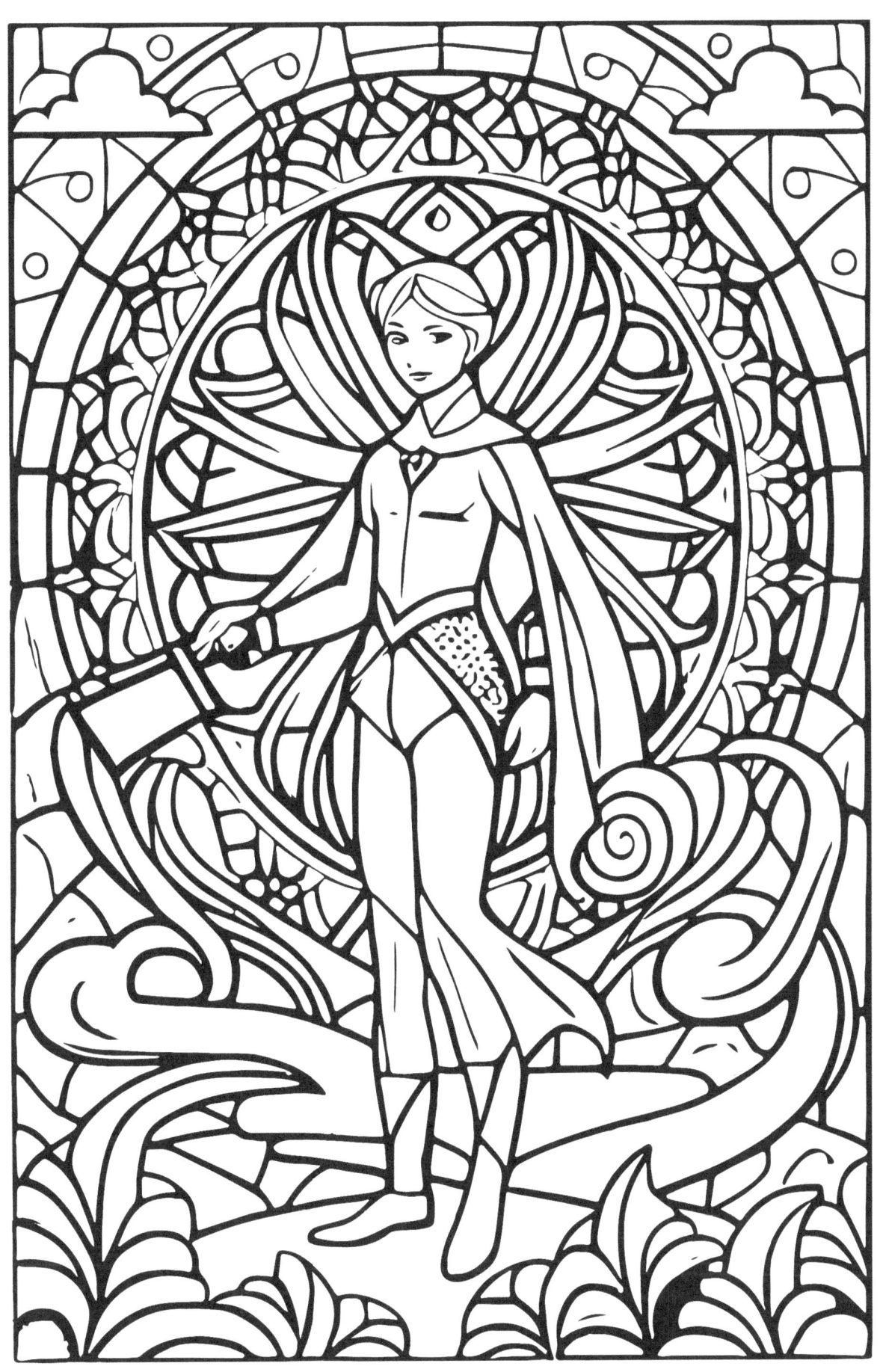

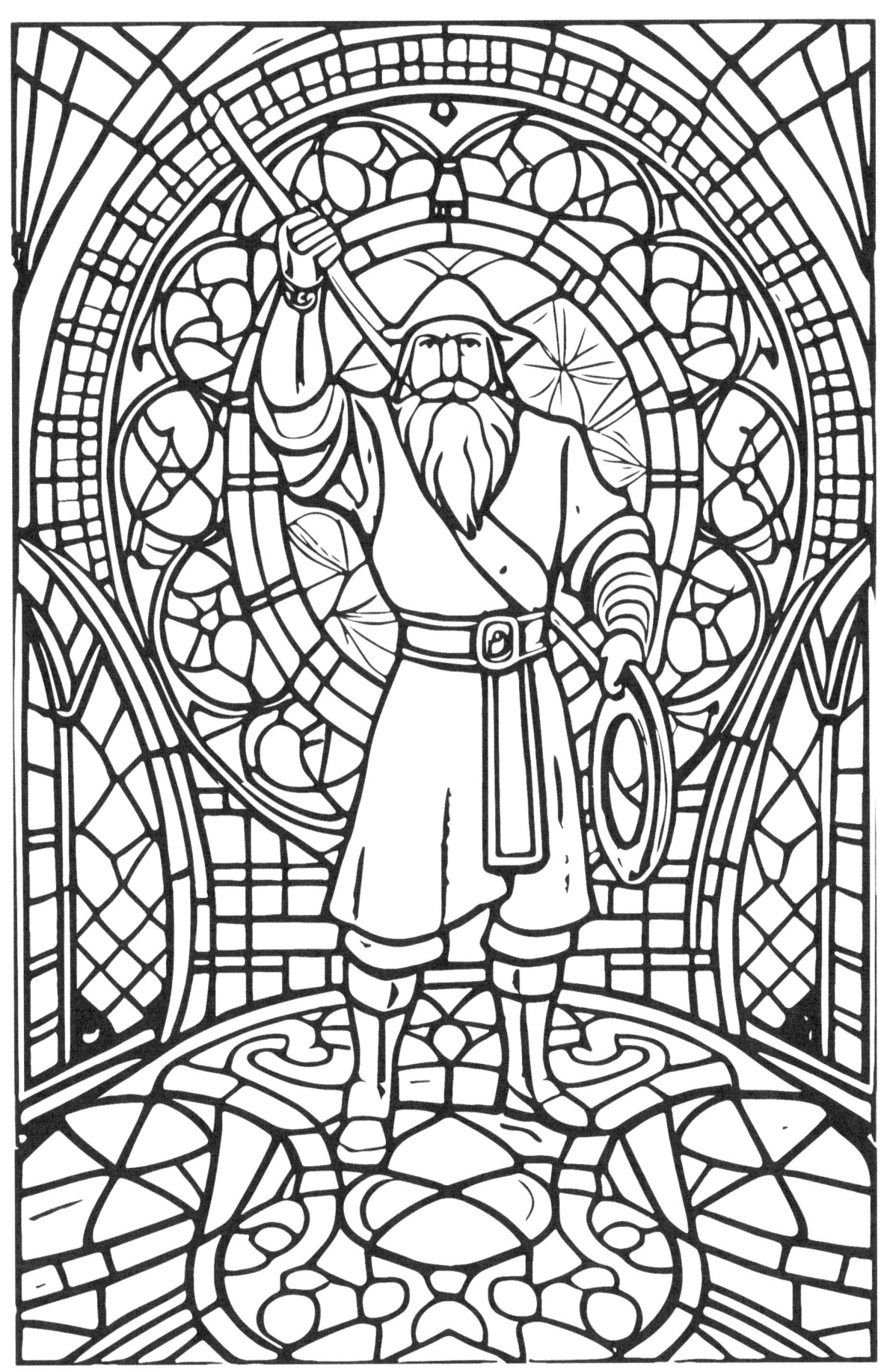

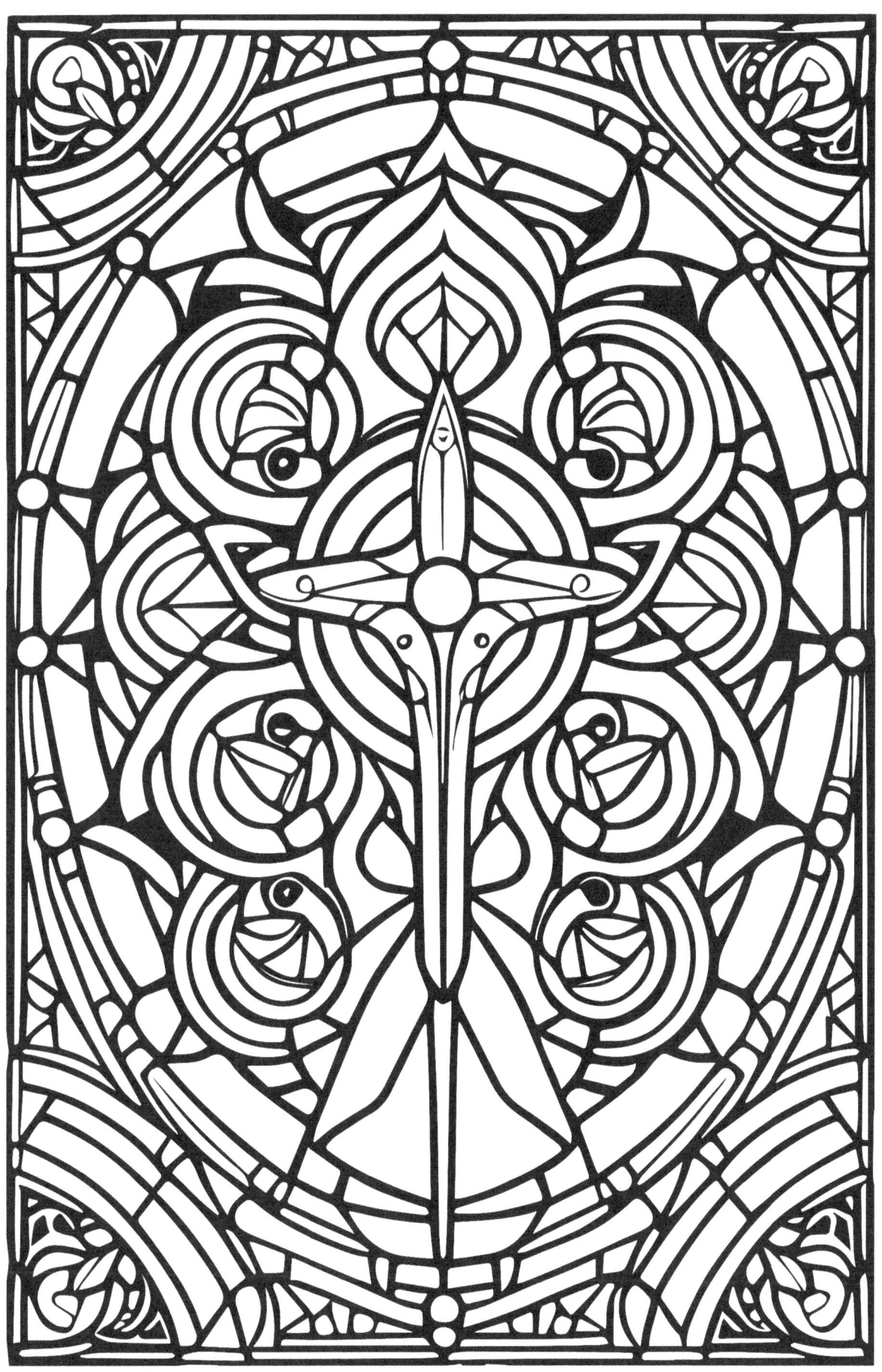

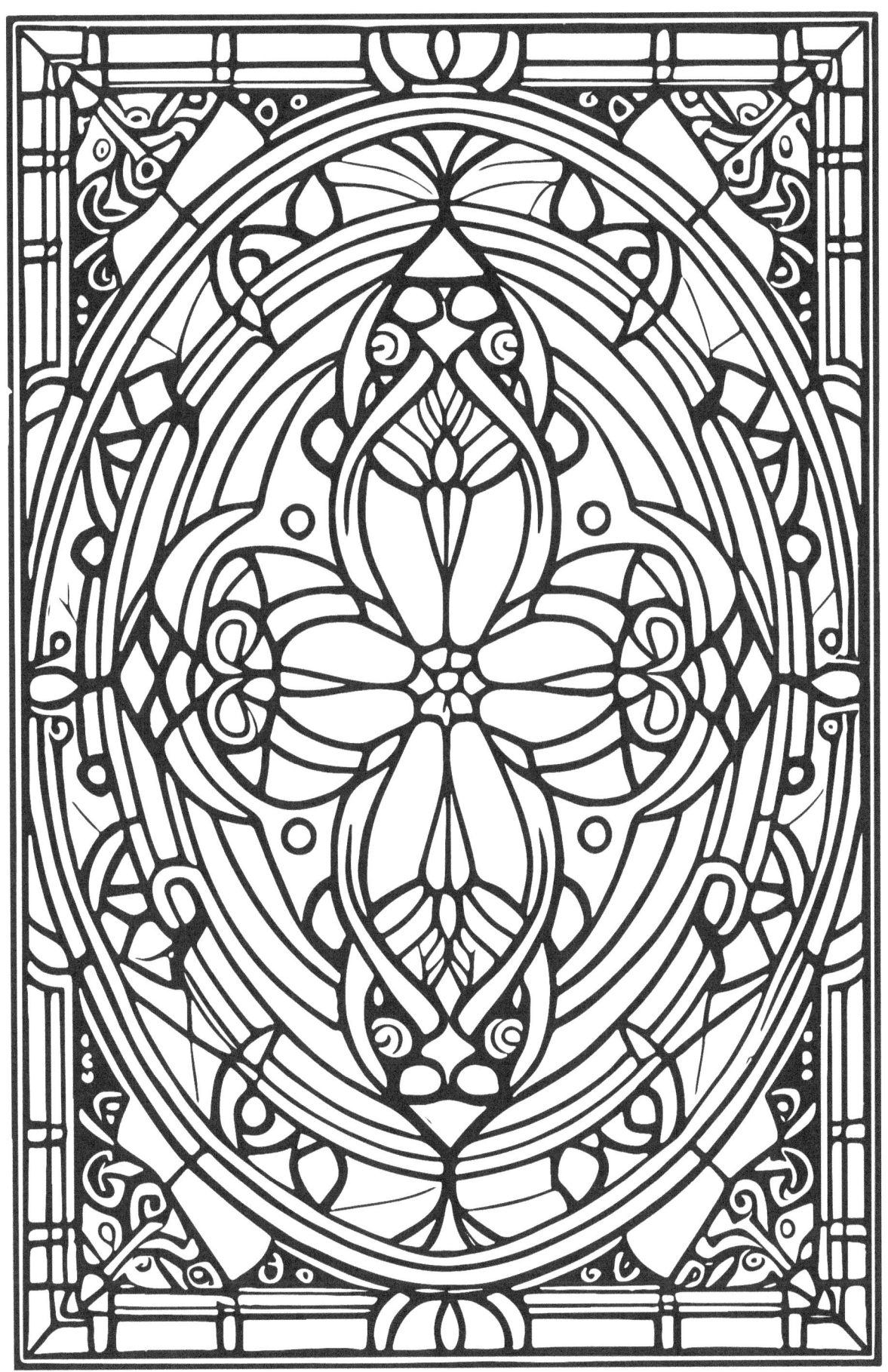

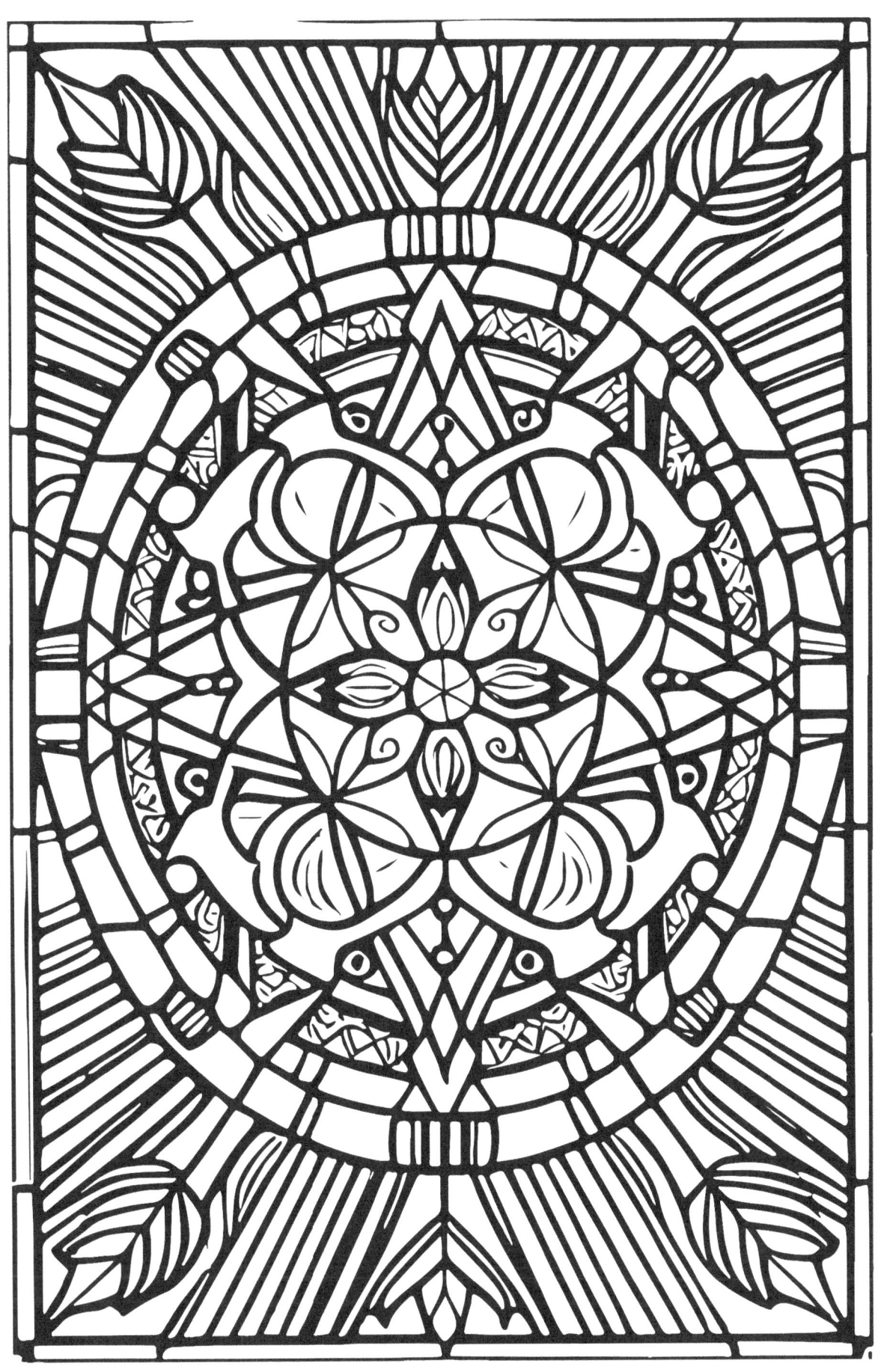

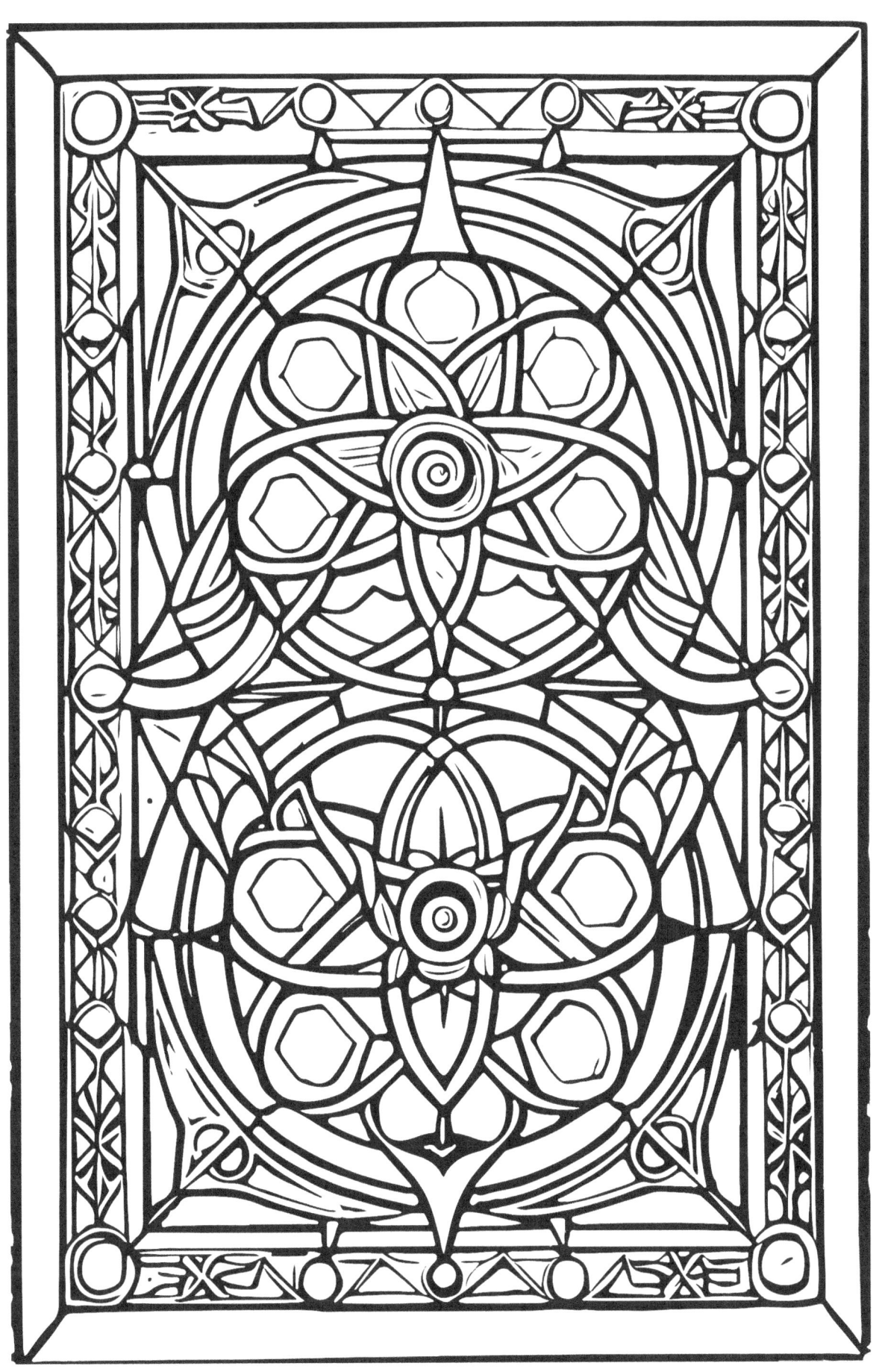

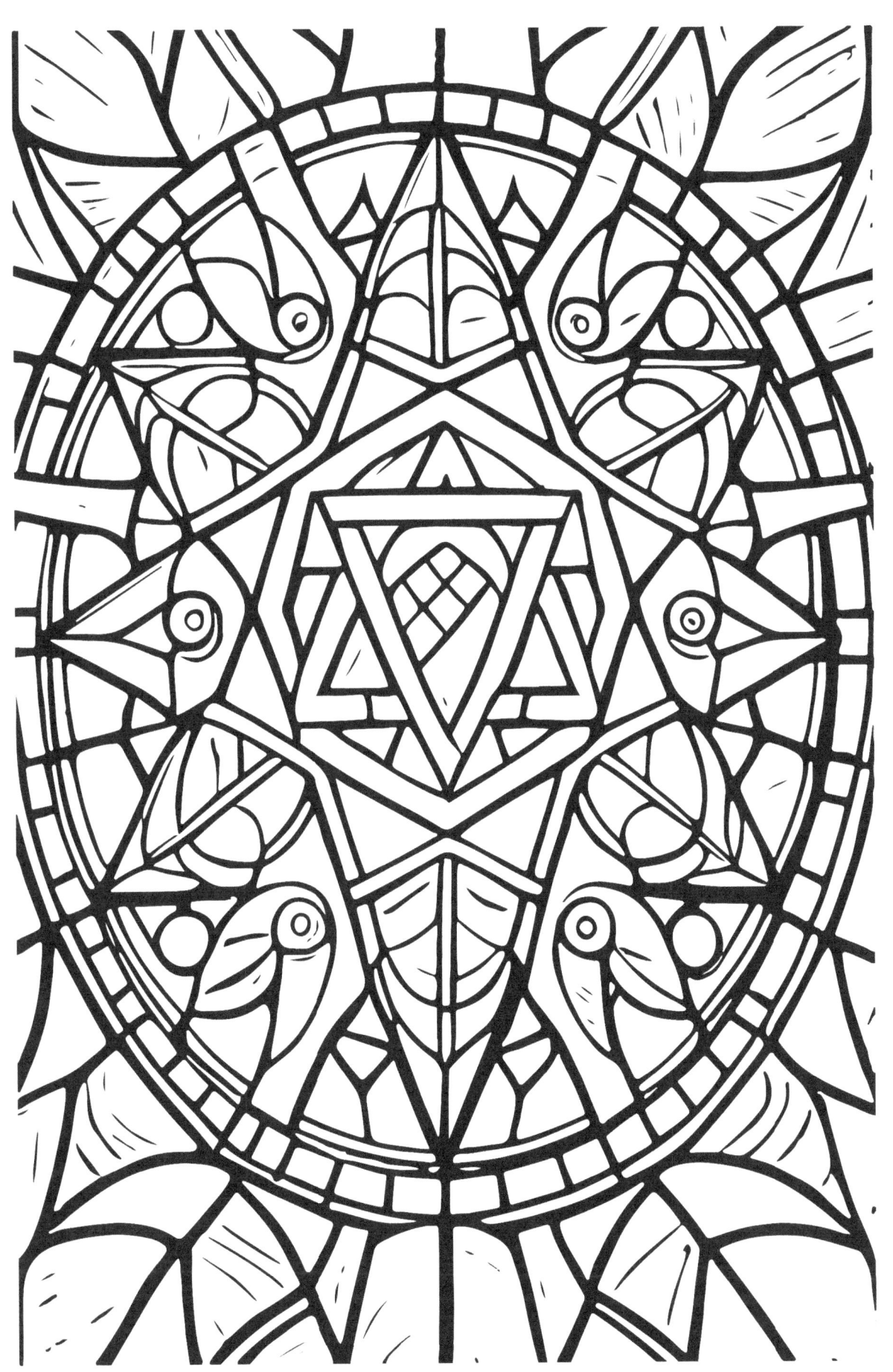

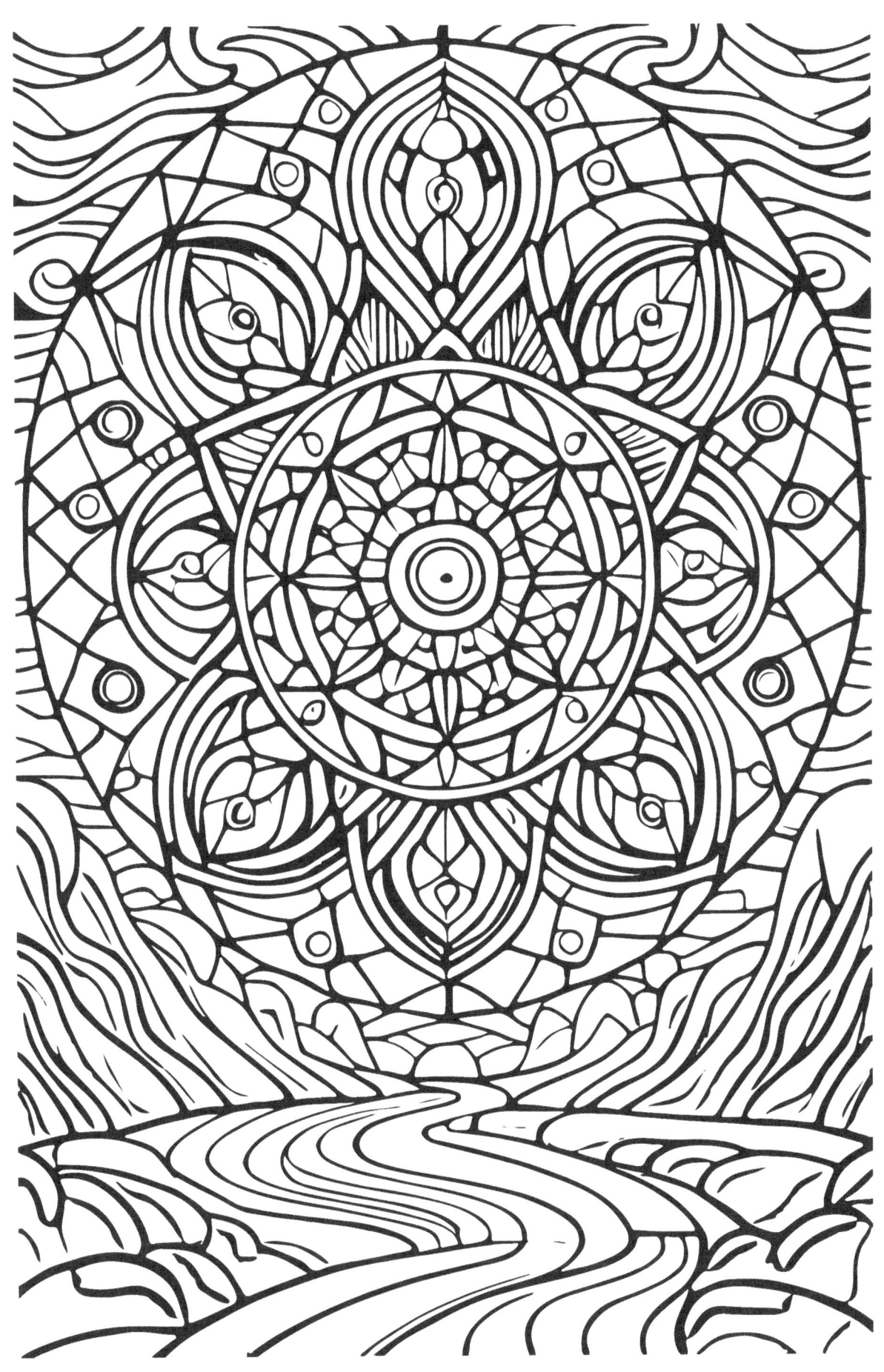

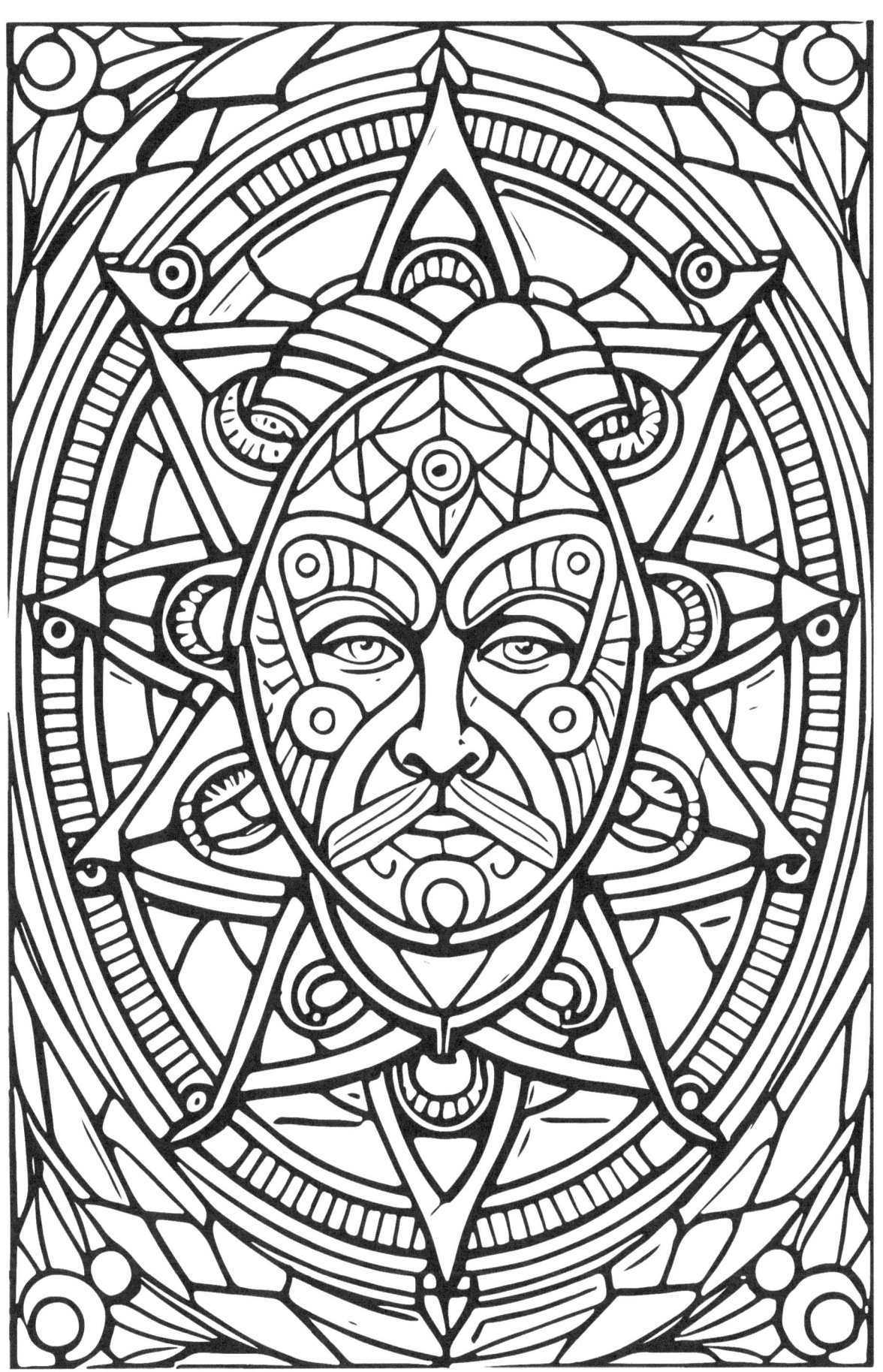

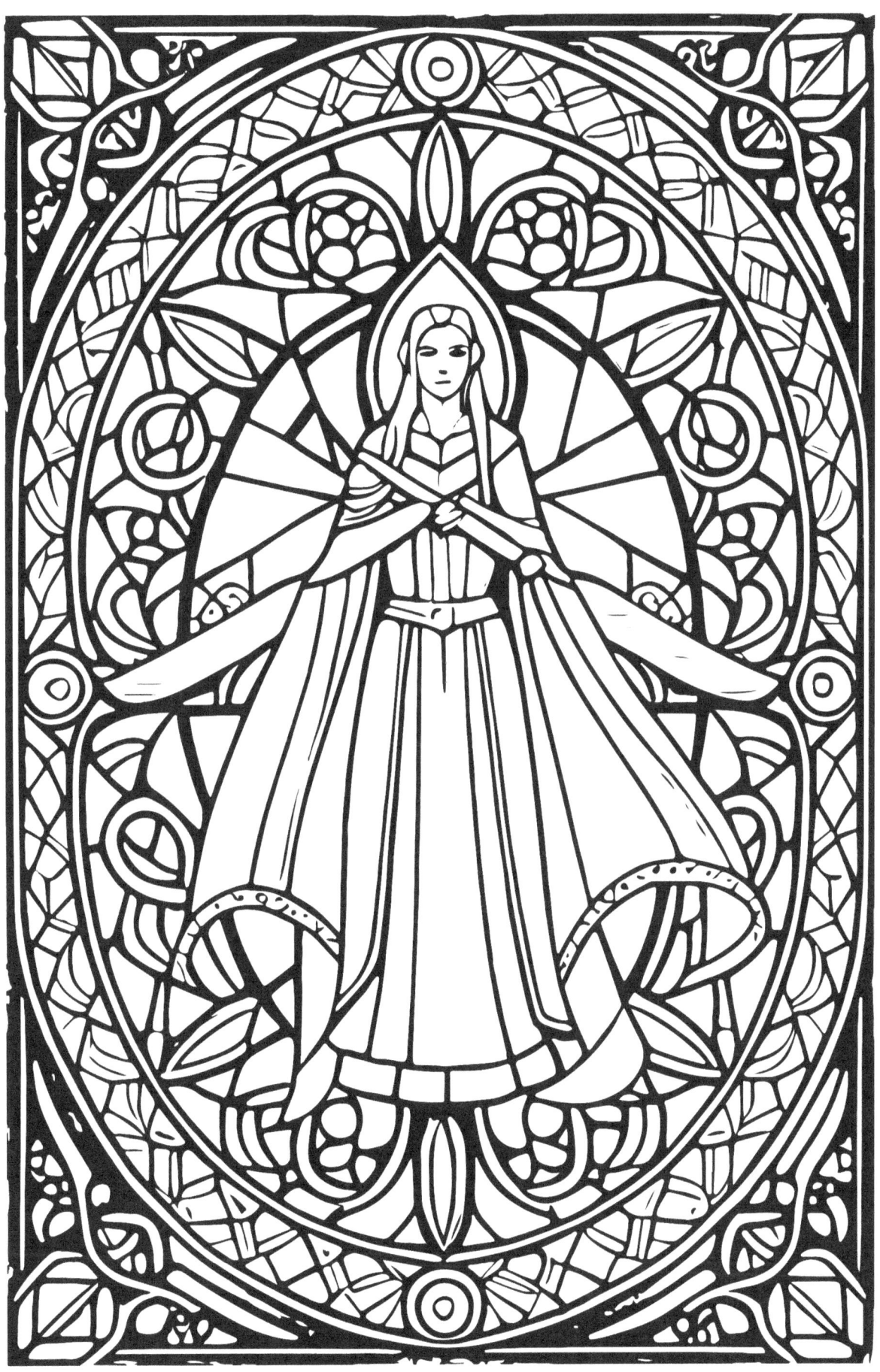

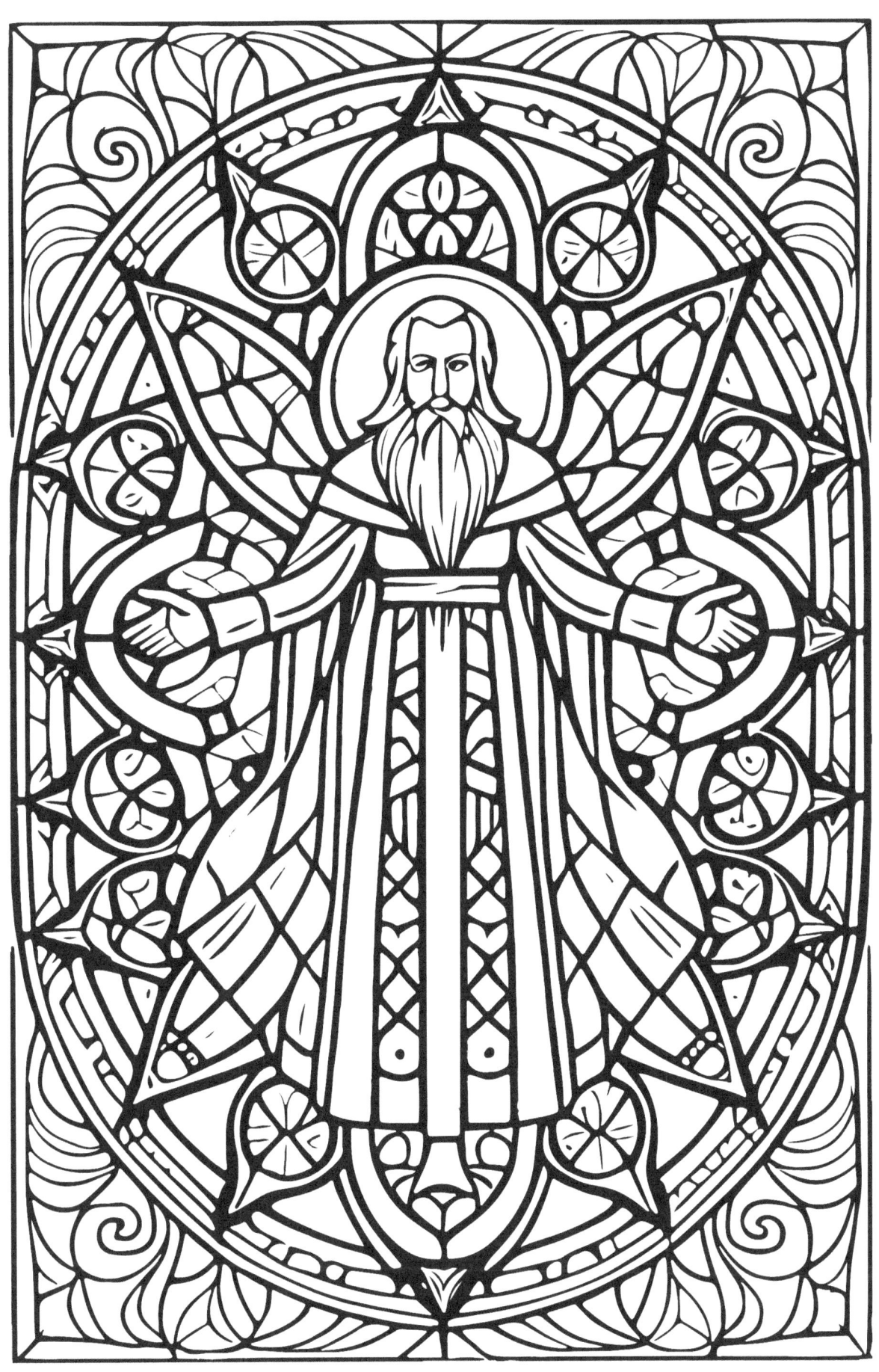

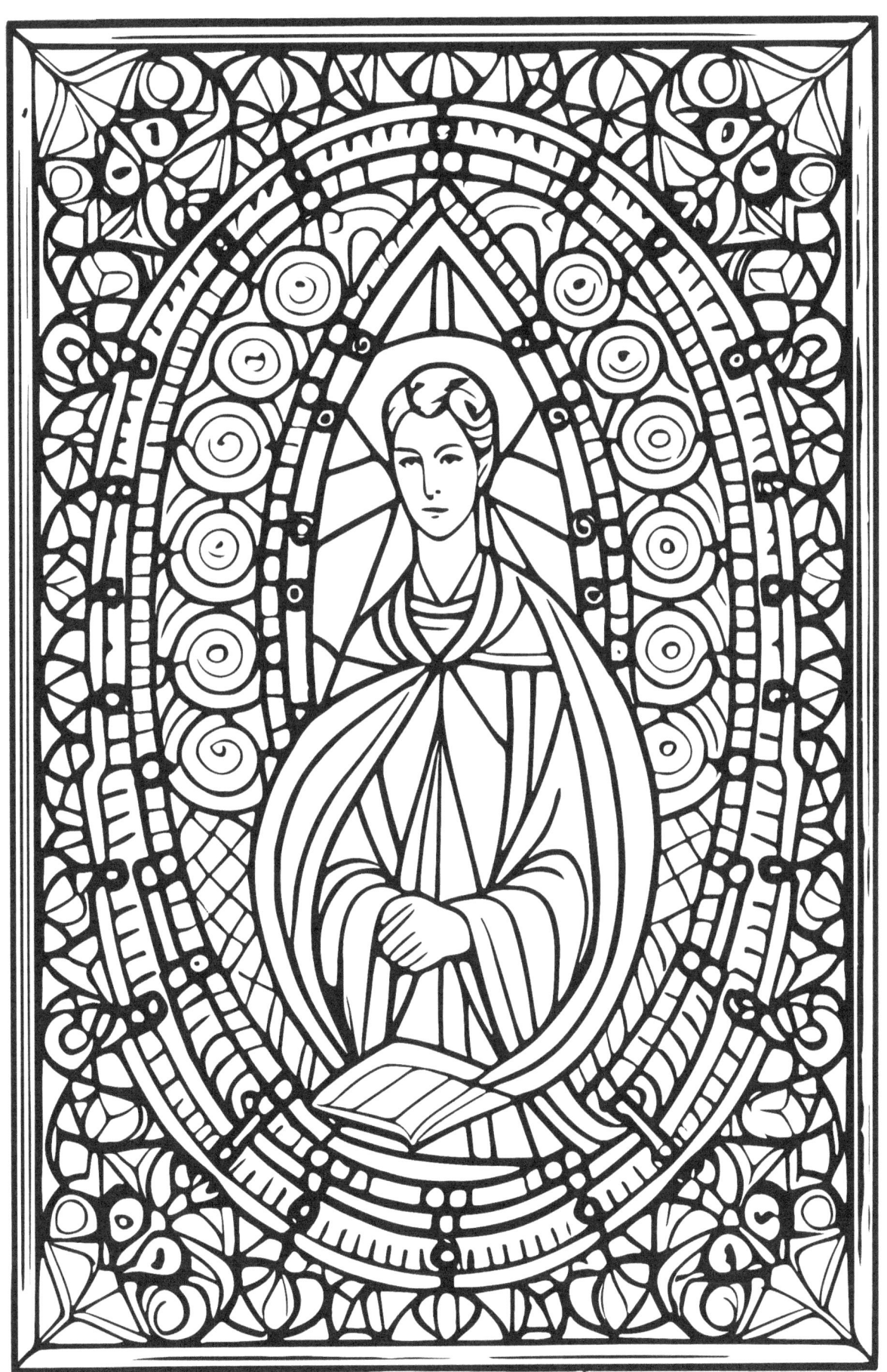

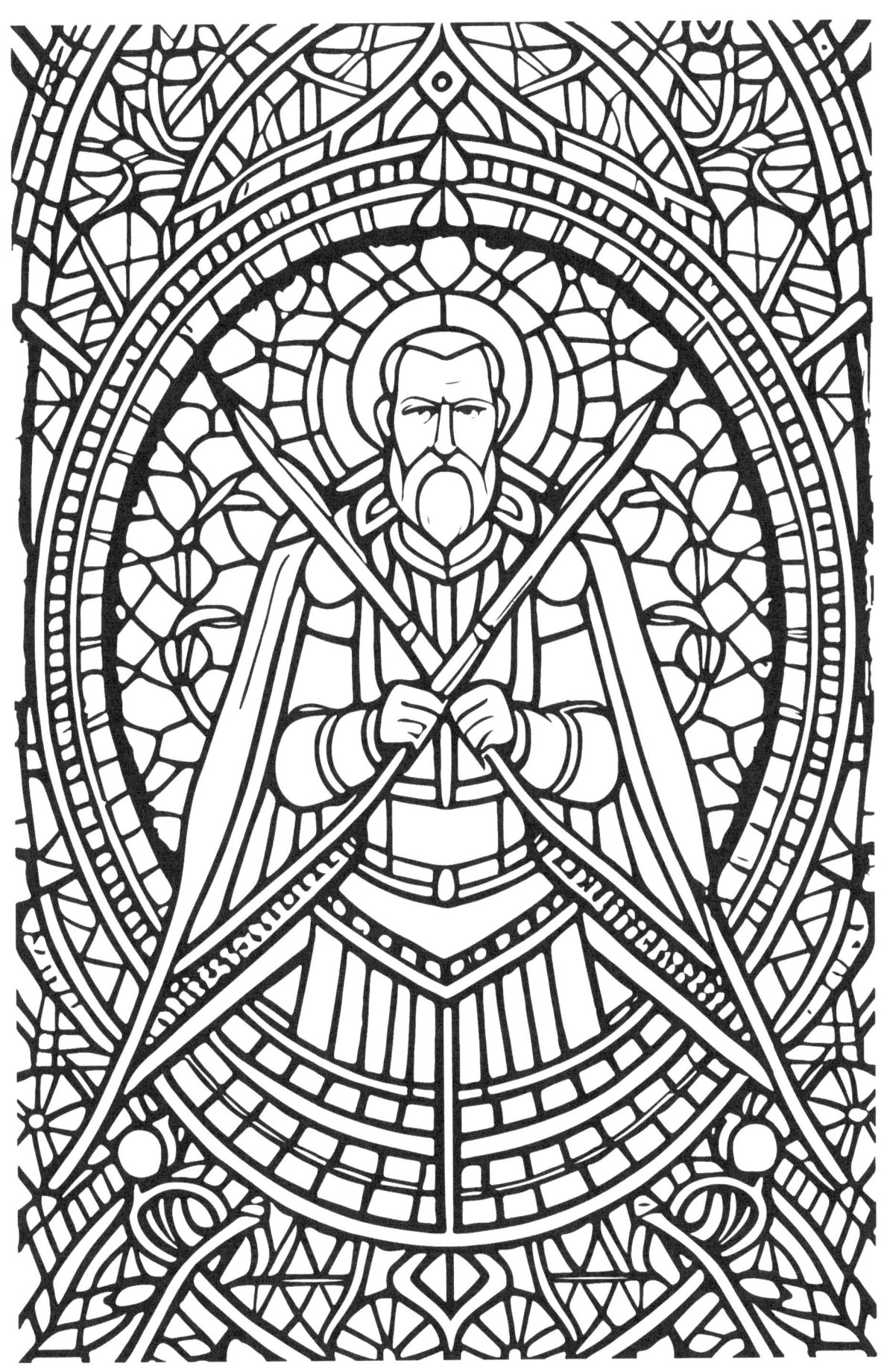

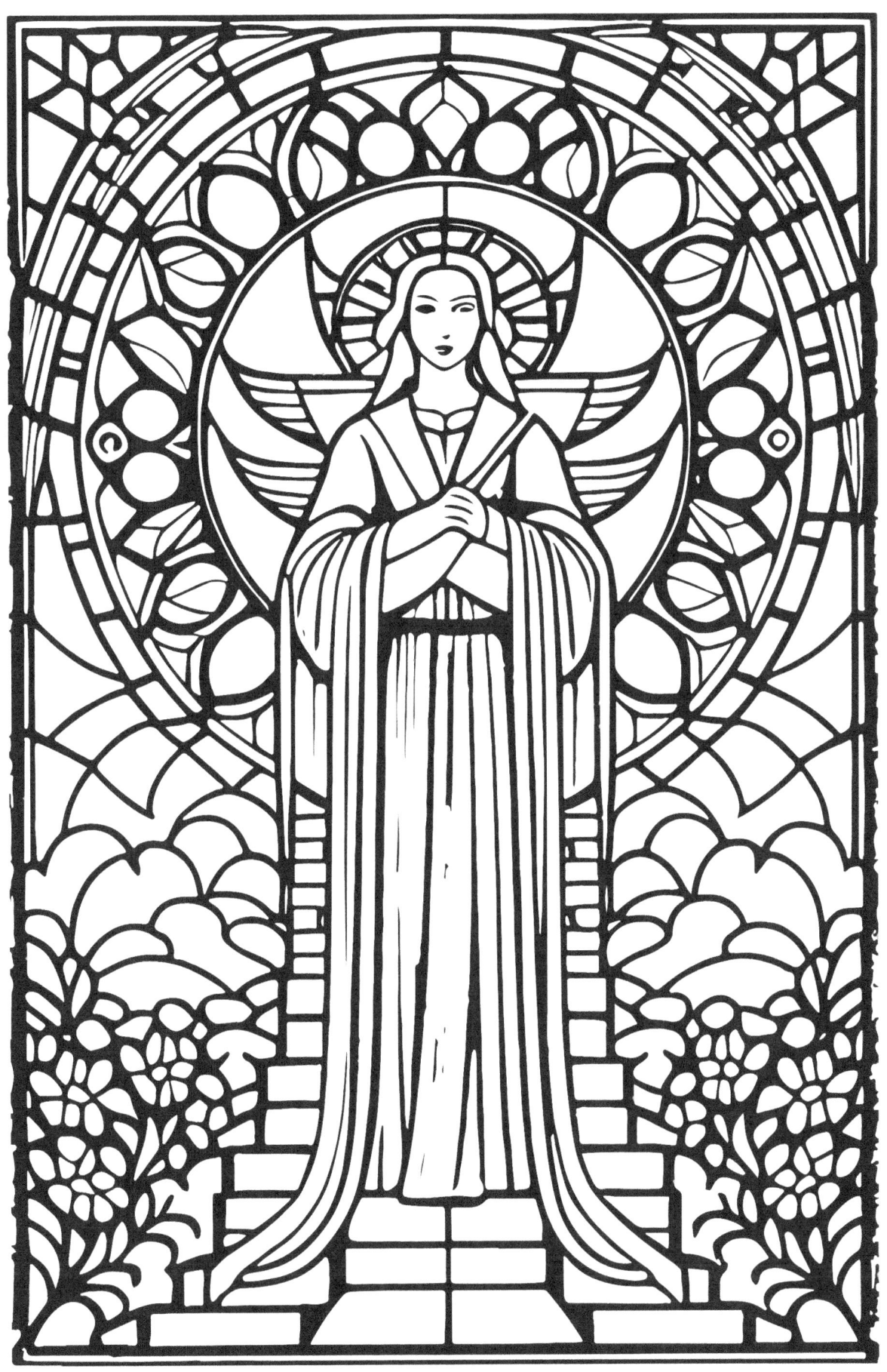

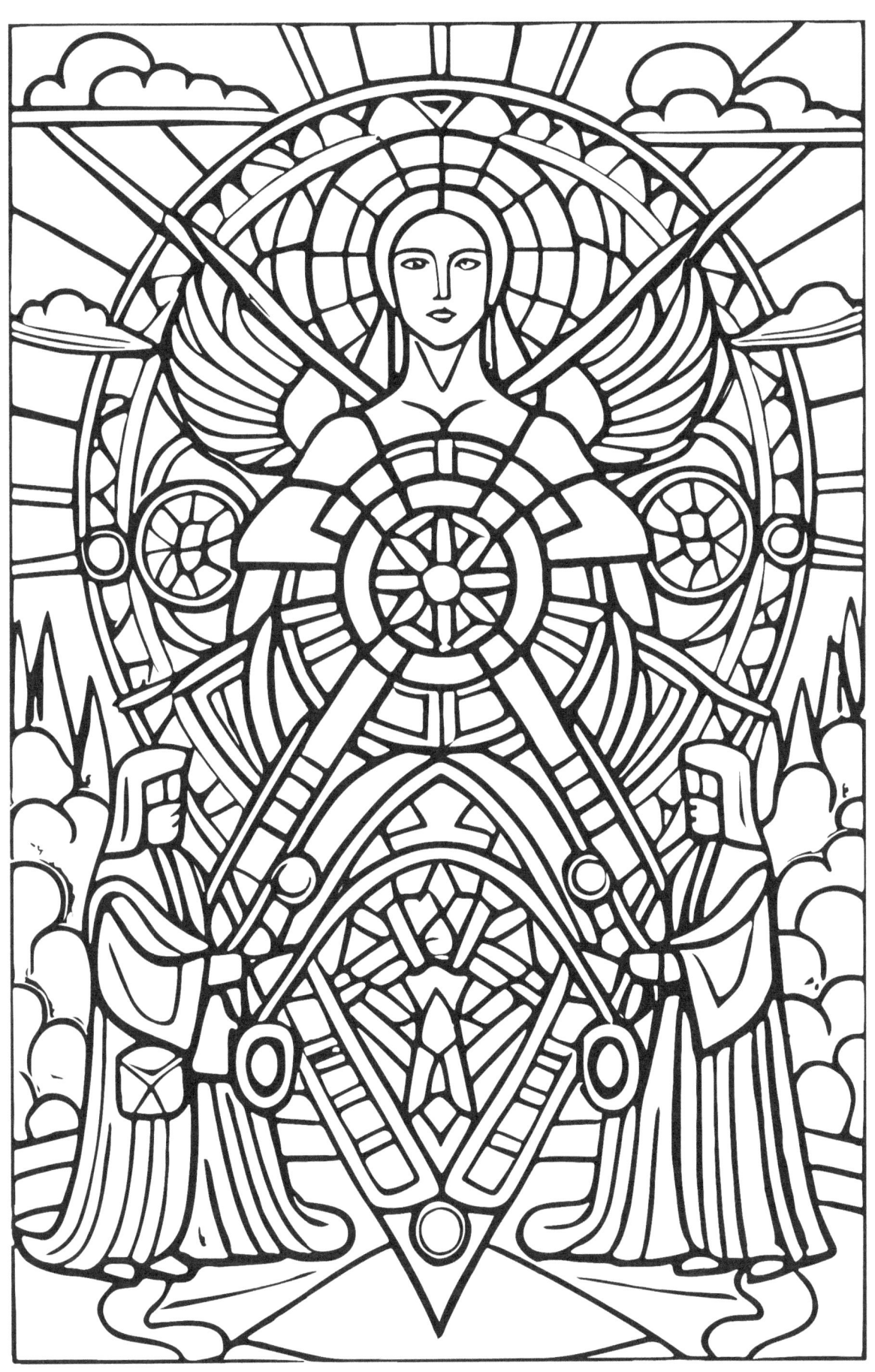

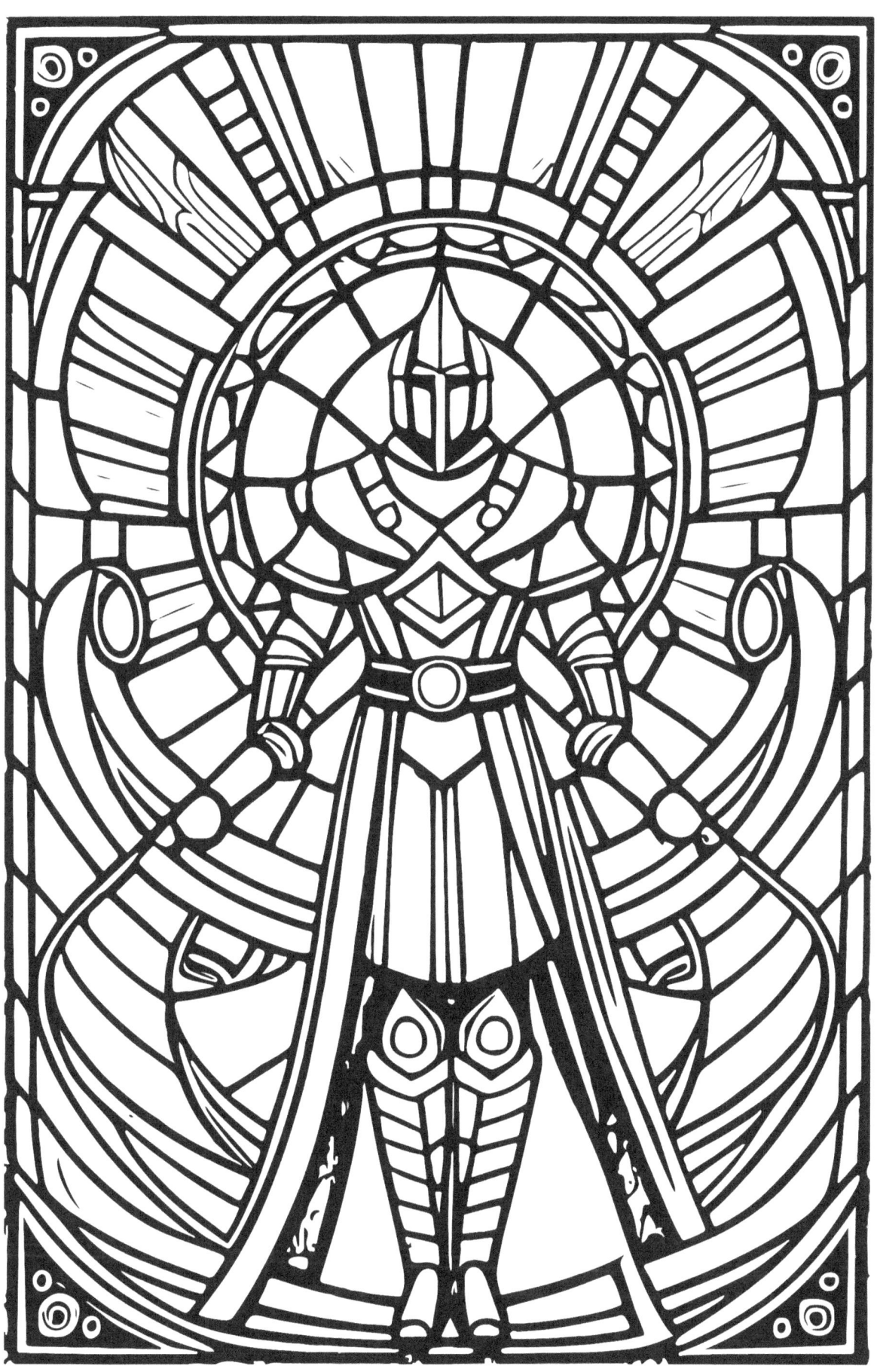

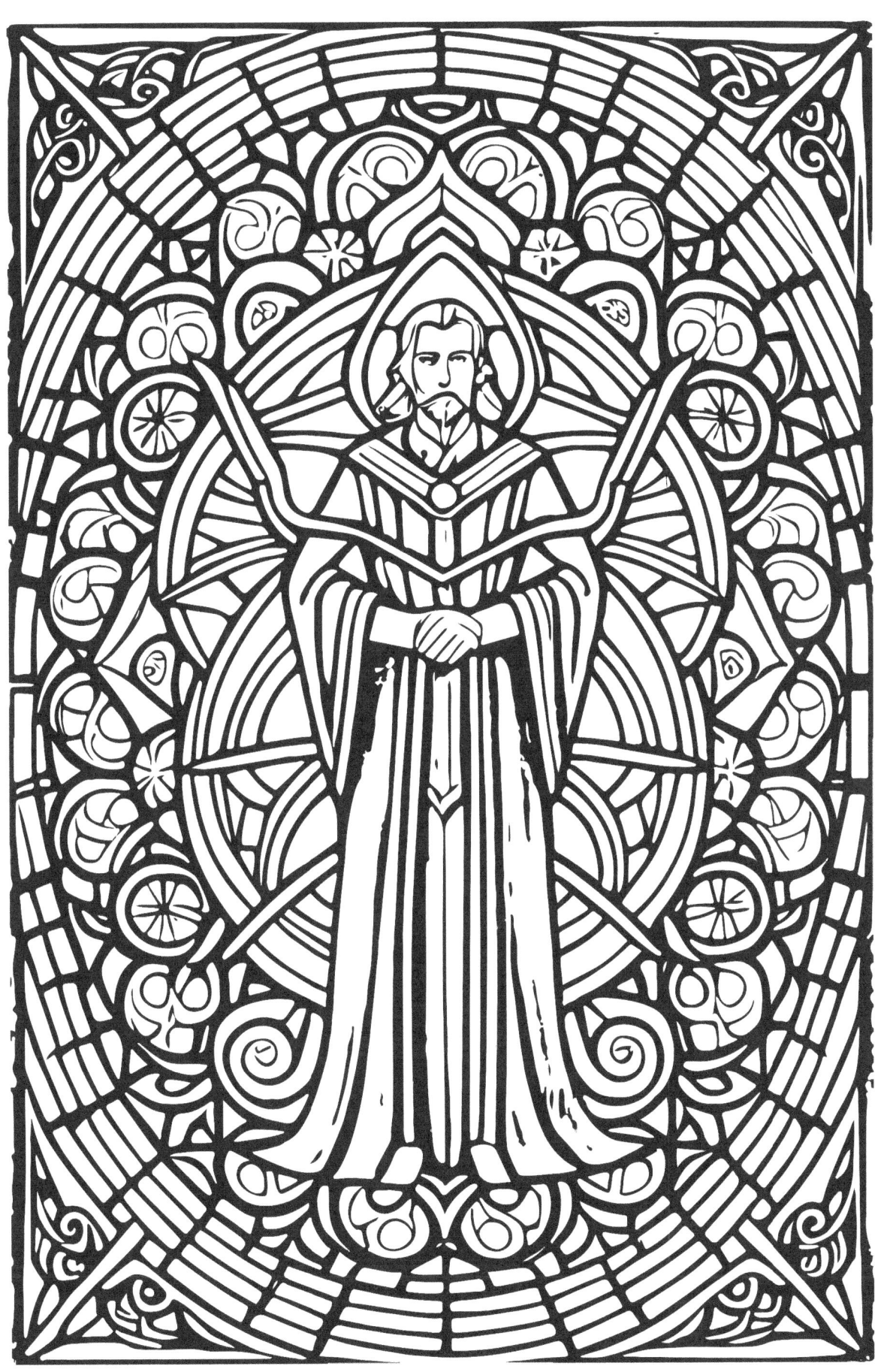

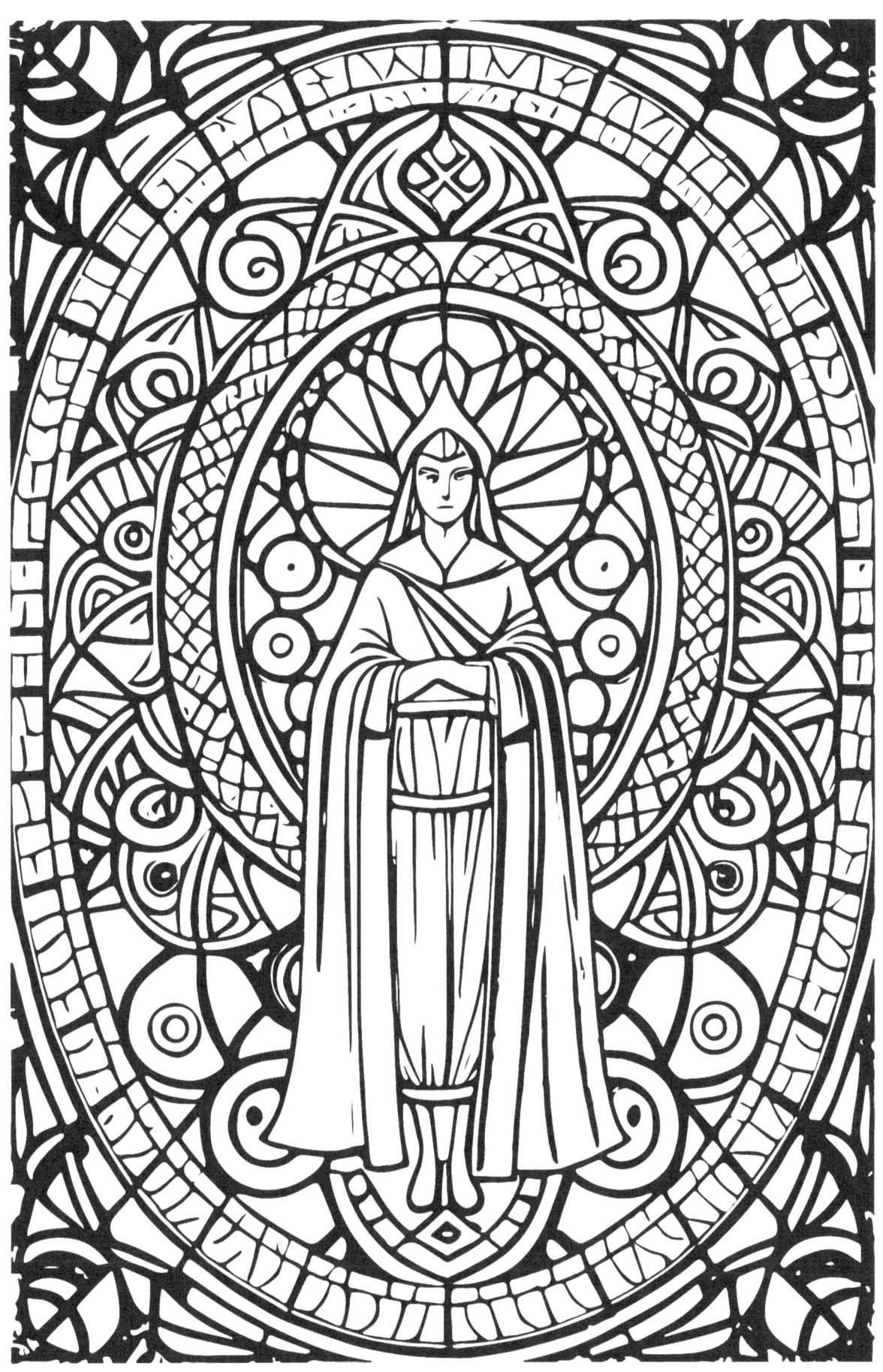

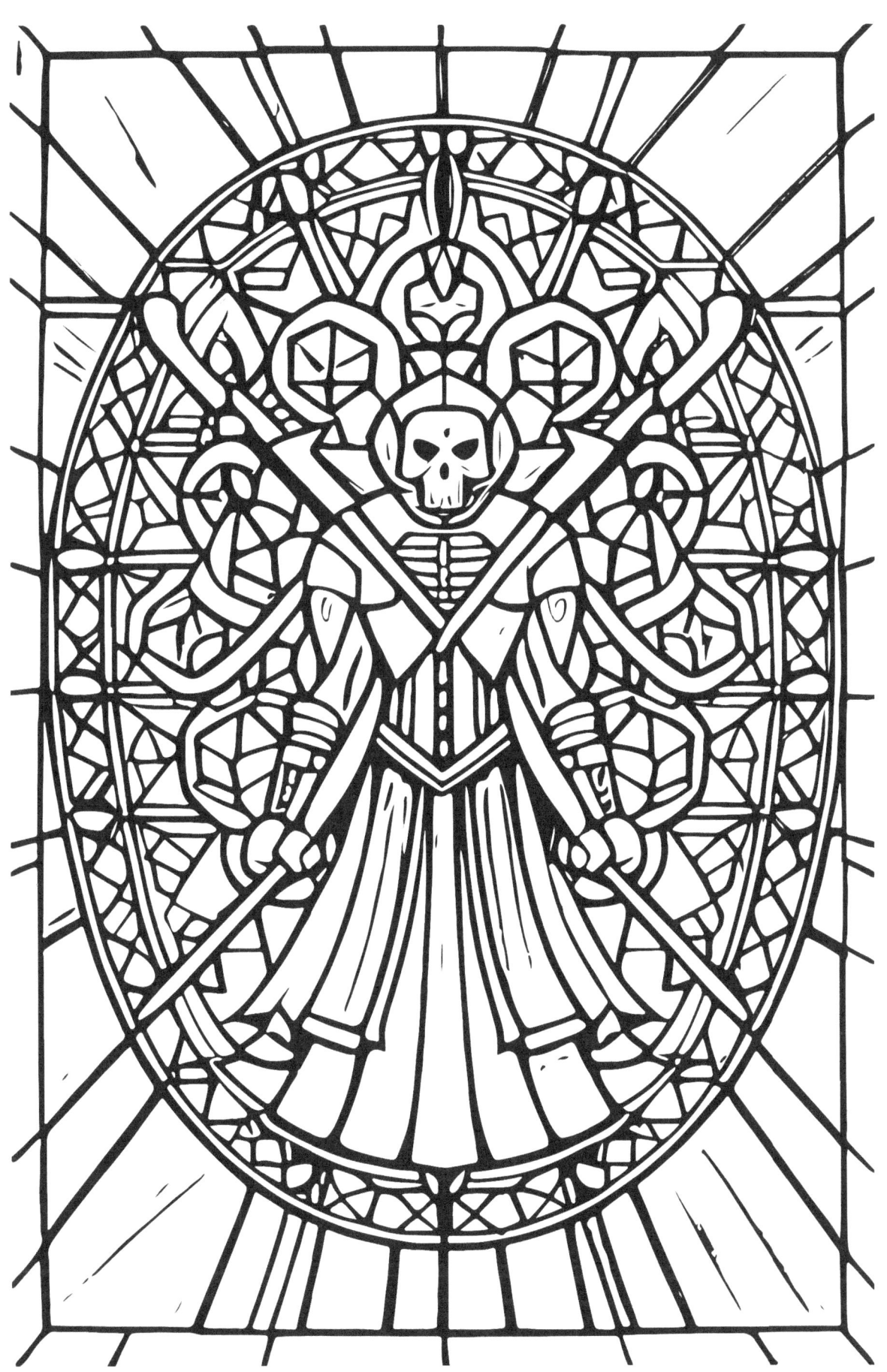

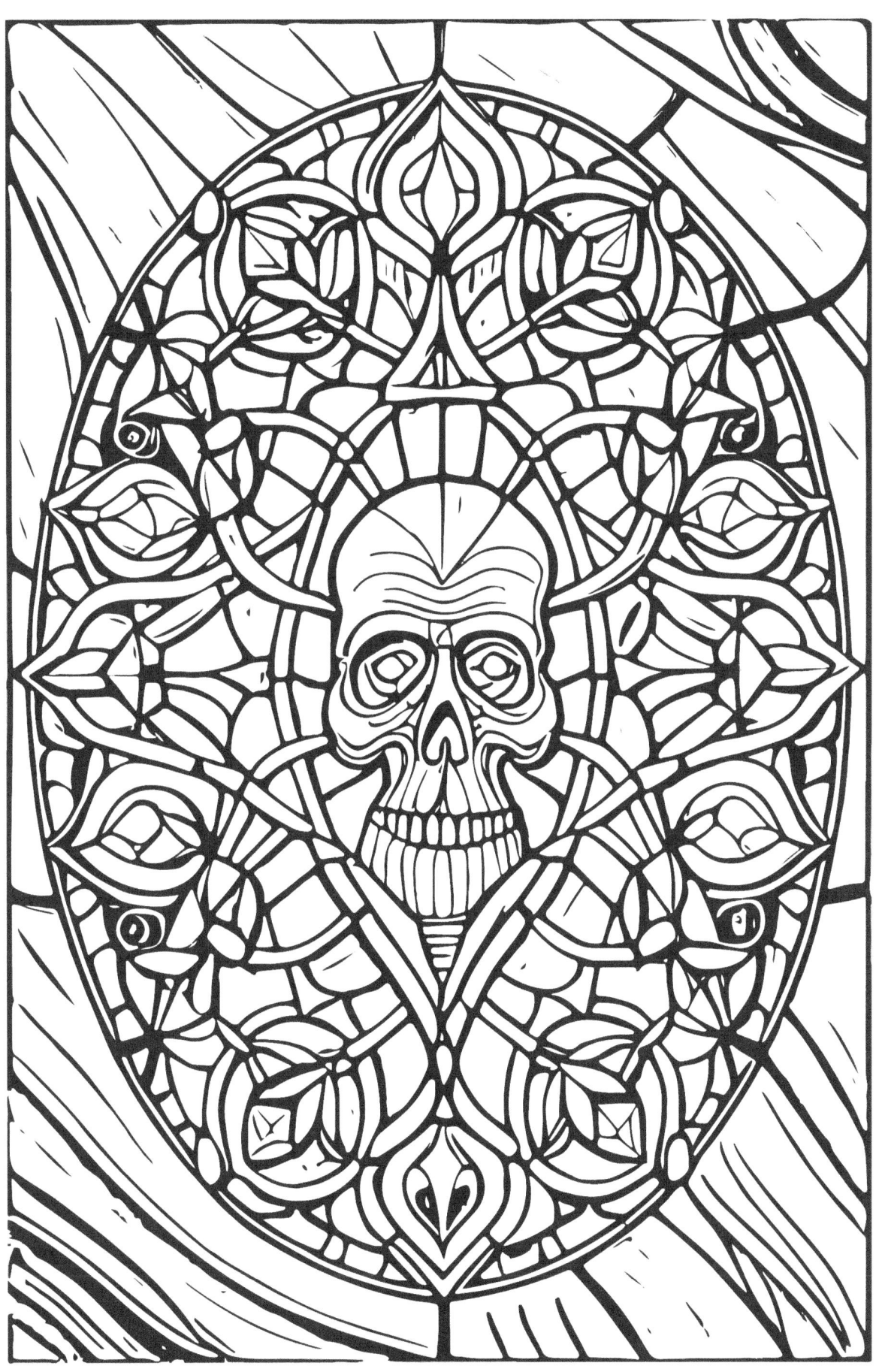

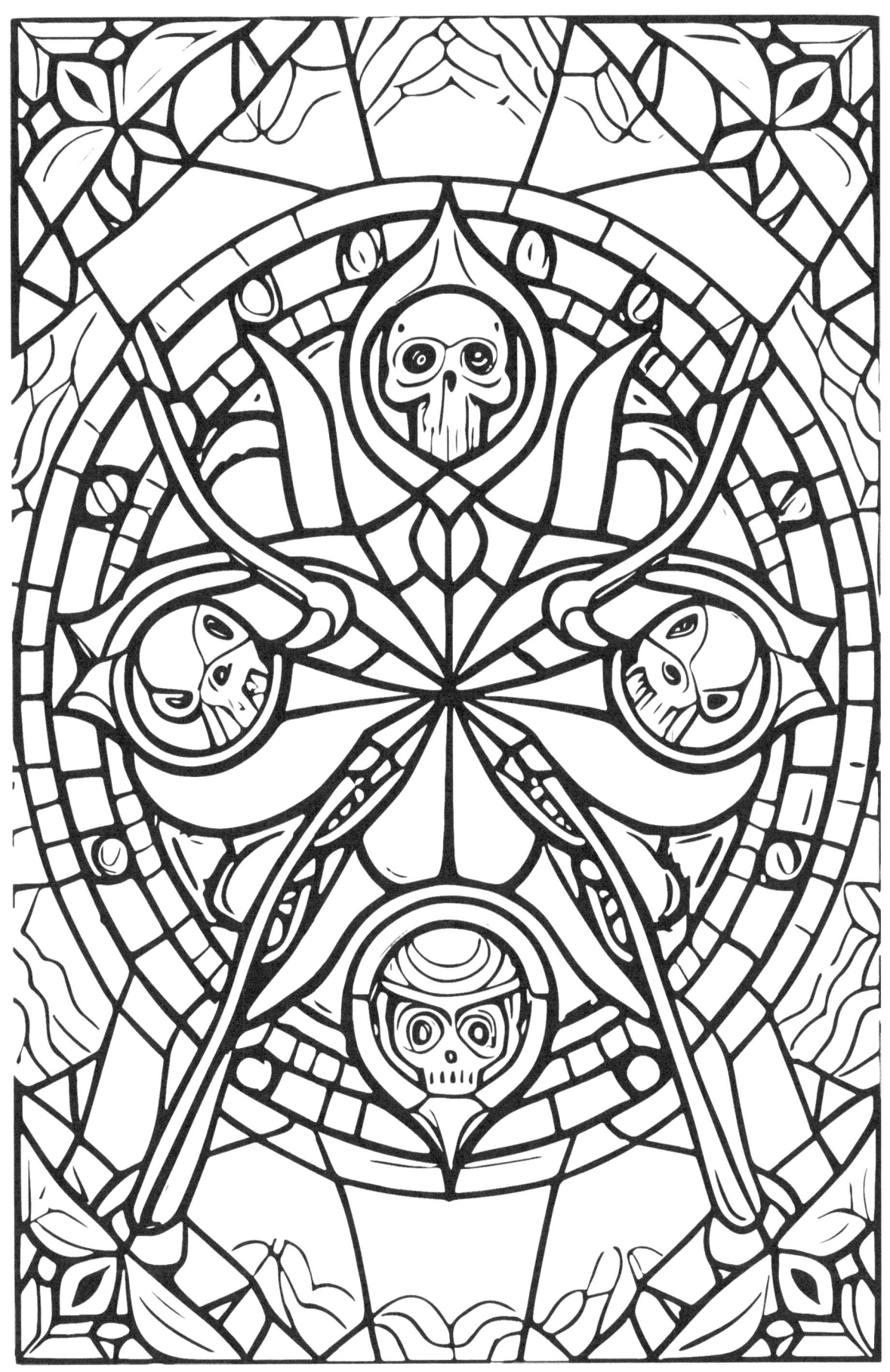

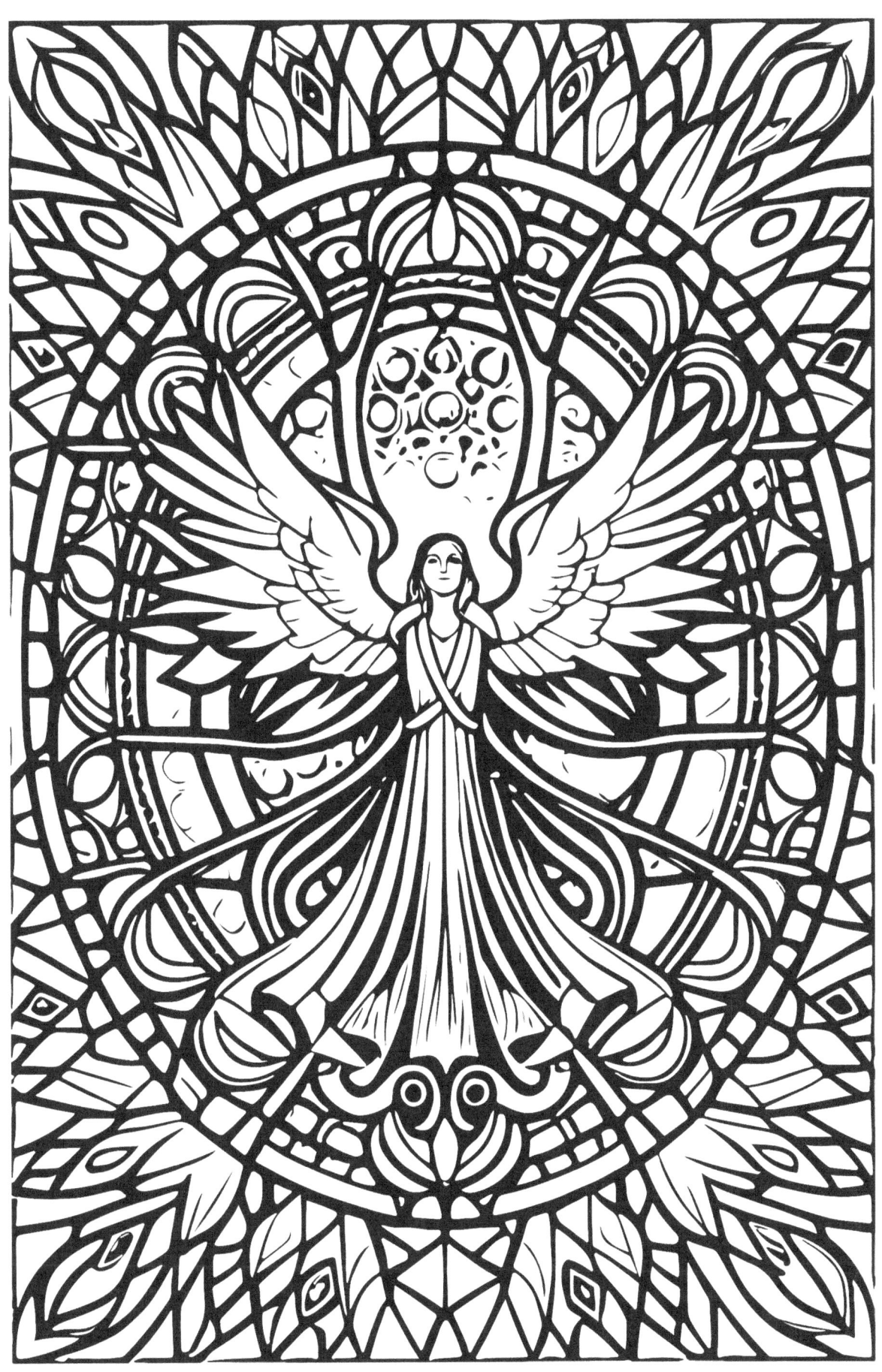

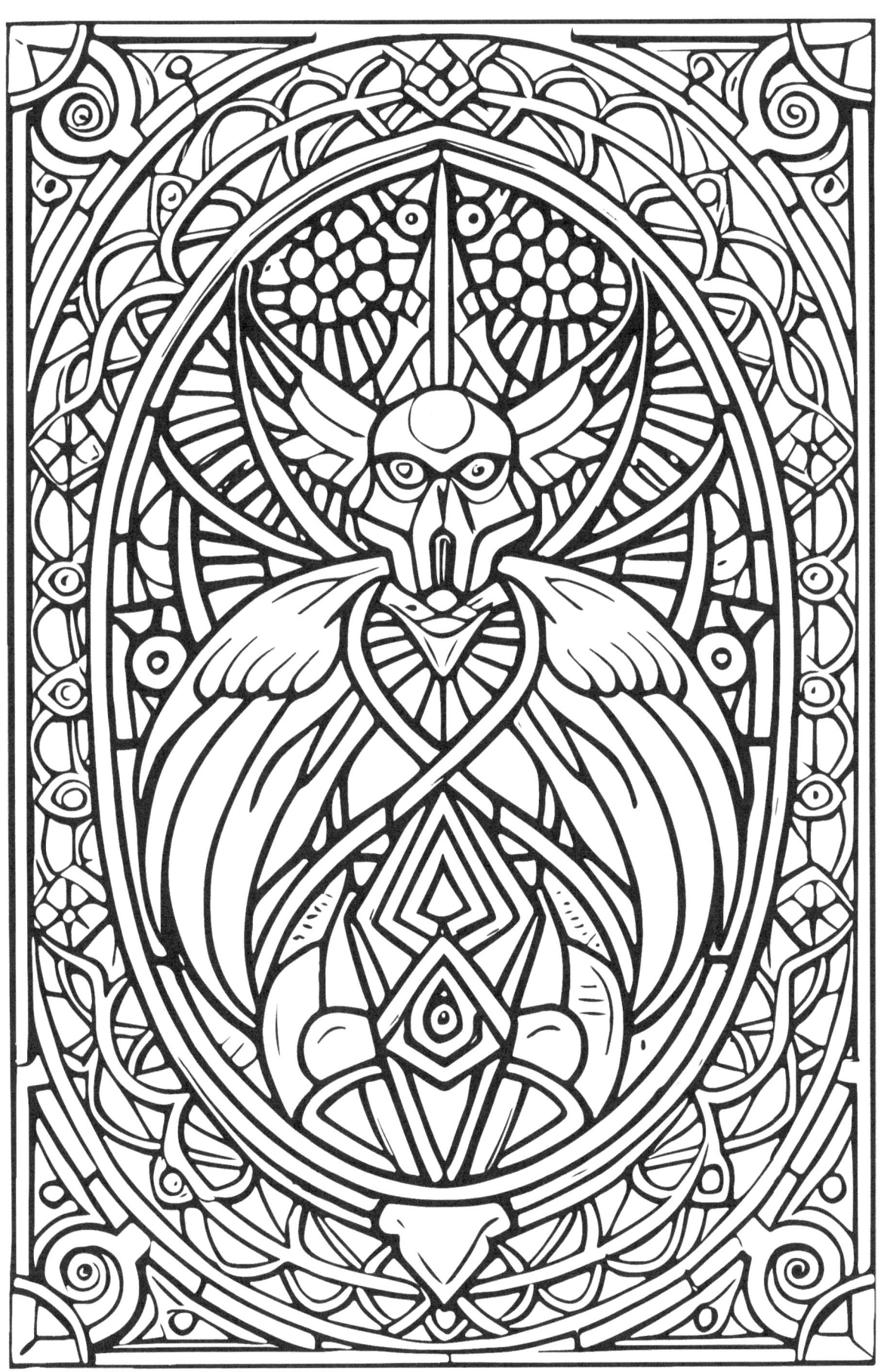

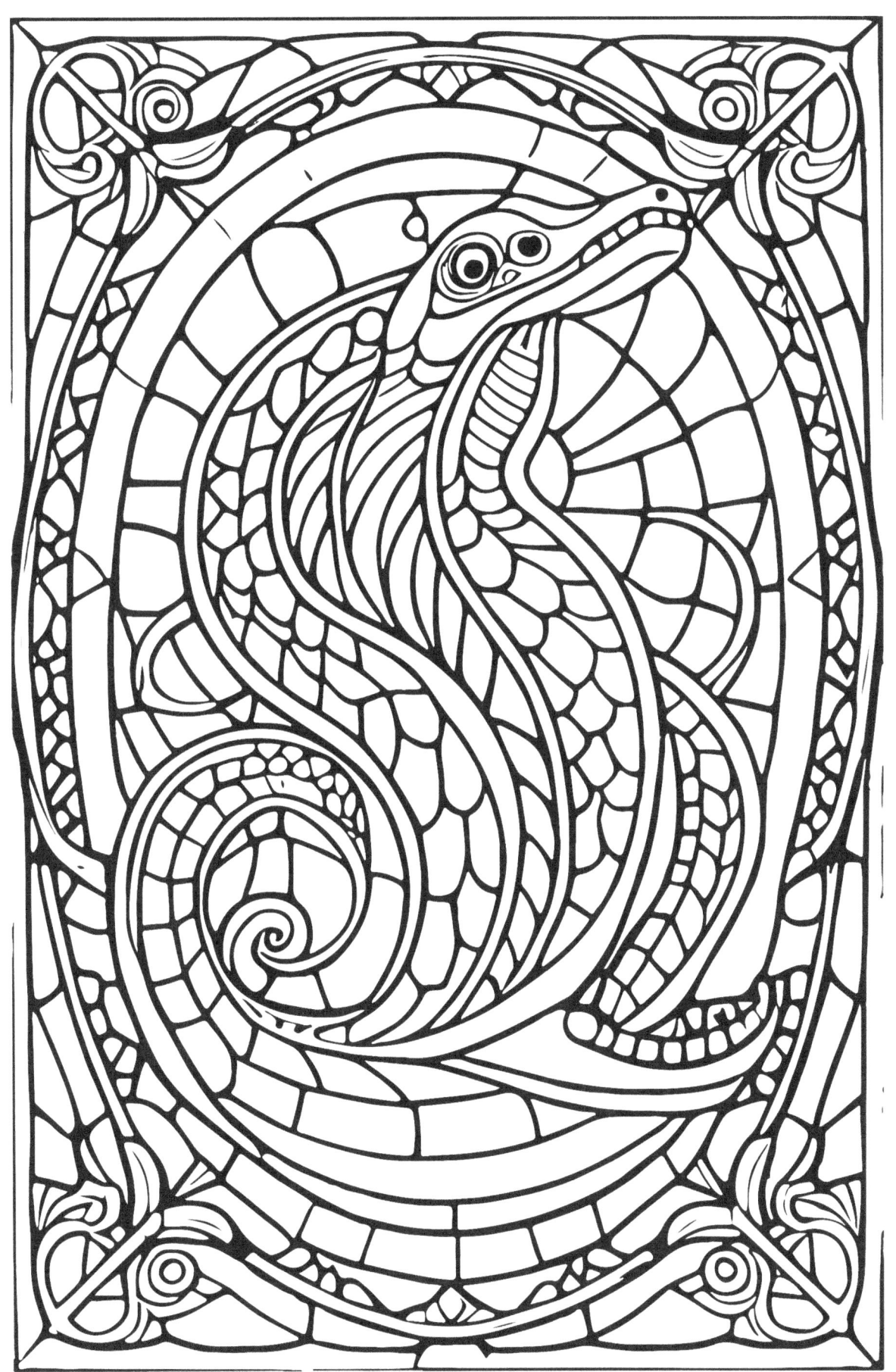

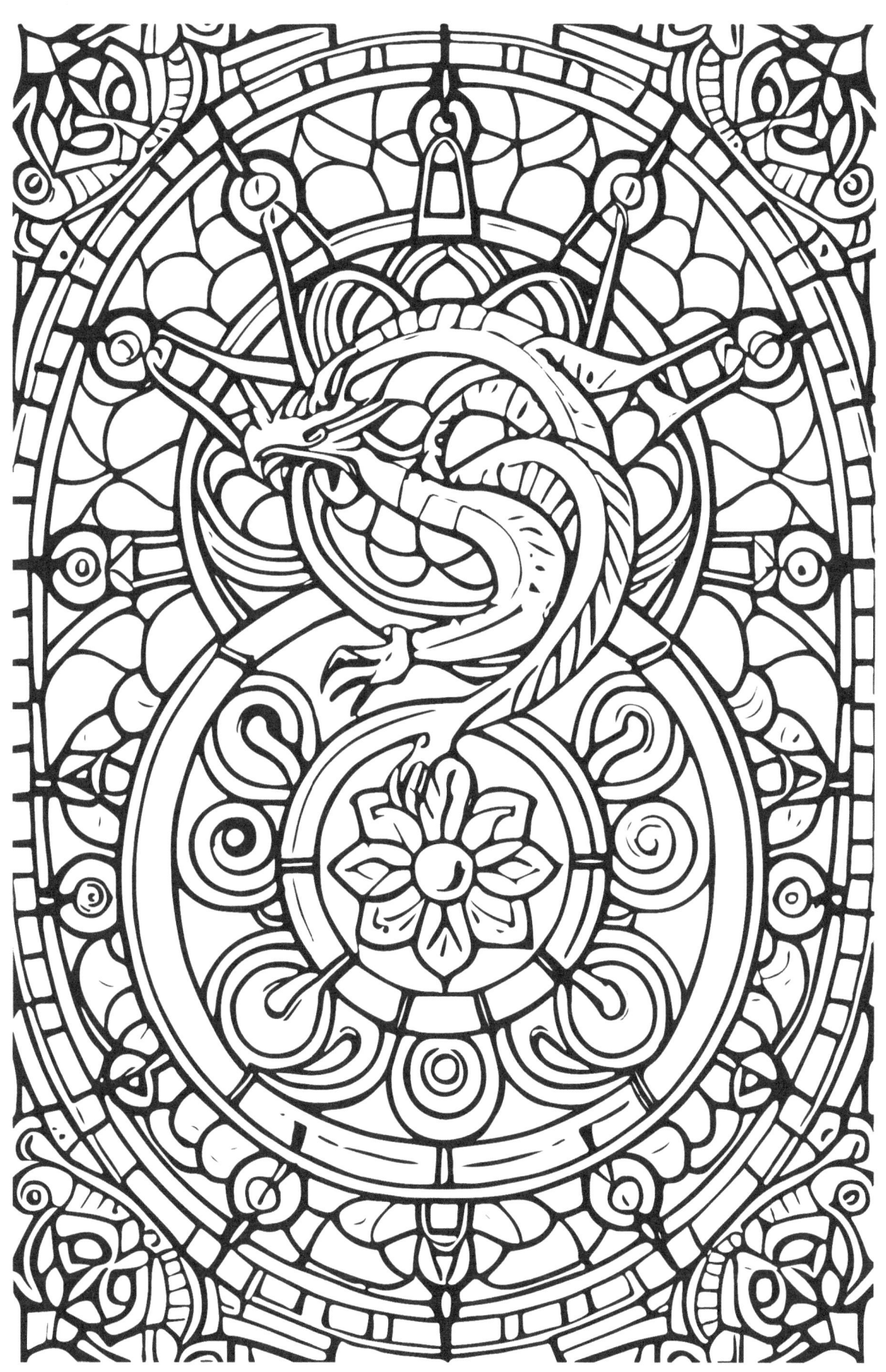

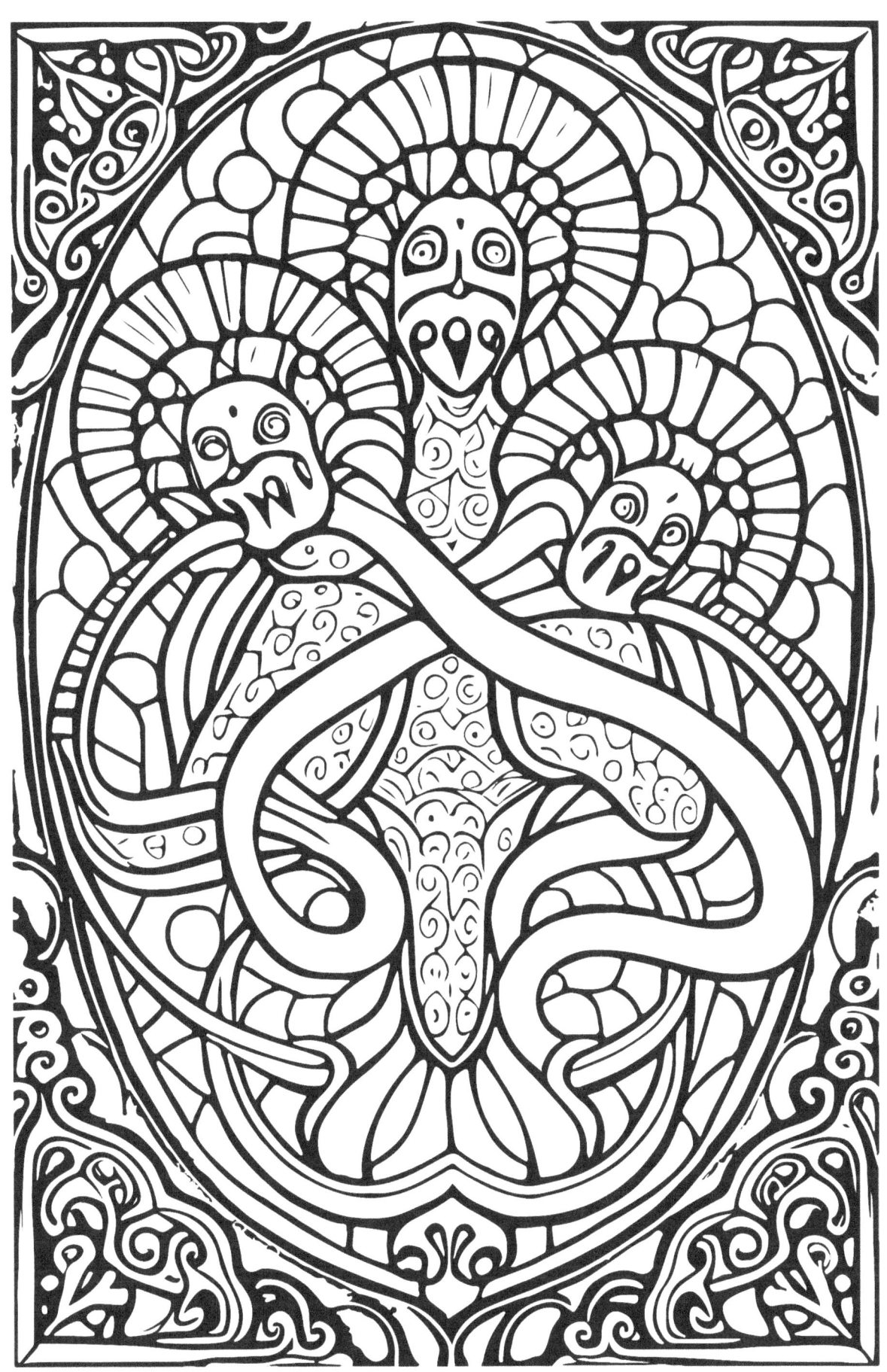

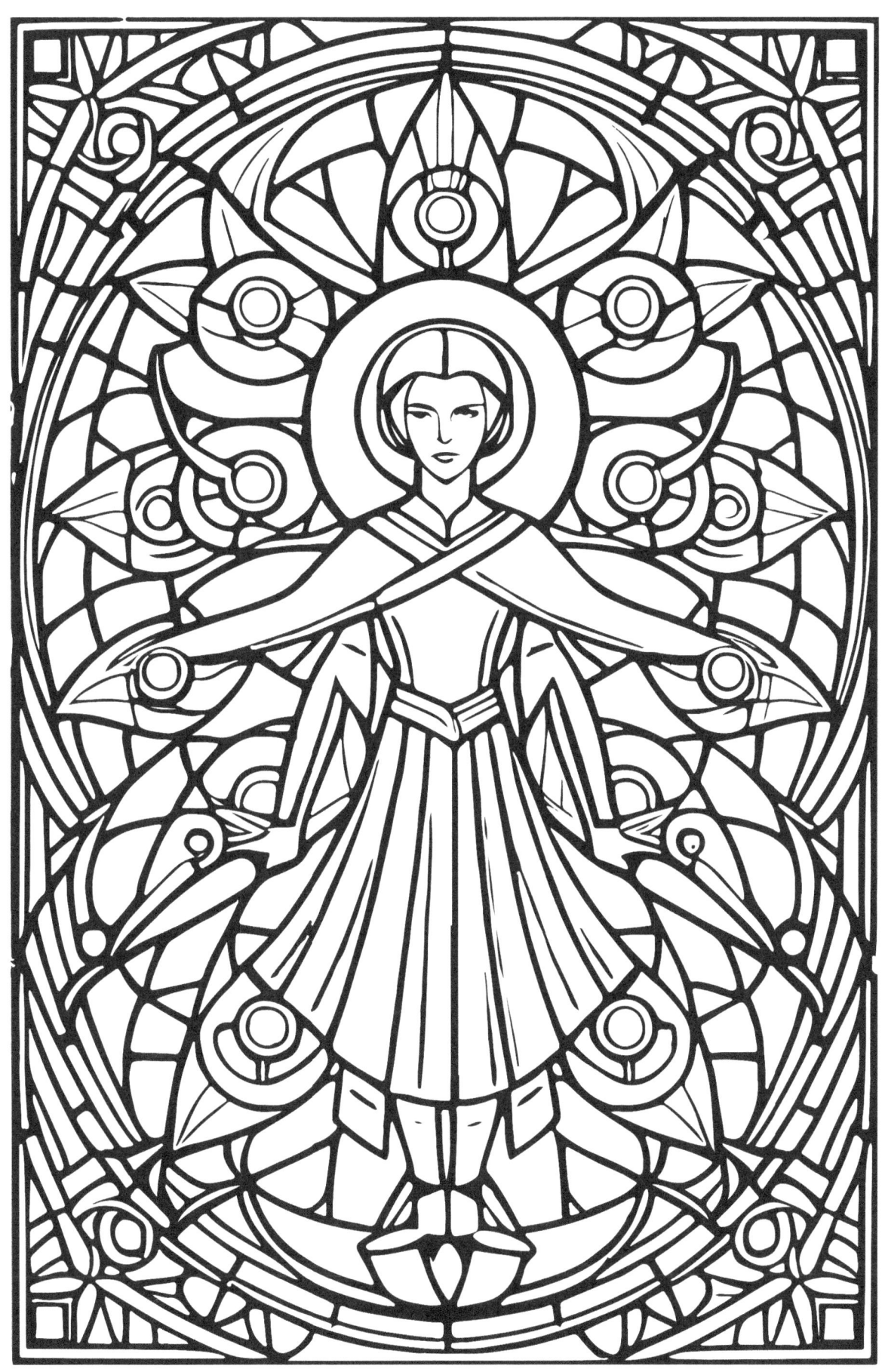

INDEX:

1 - HEROE

2 - KNIGHT

3 - DWARF

4 - ELF

5 - HALF-GIANT

6 - SWORD

7 - SHIELD

8 - ARROWS

9 - GRIMOIRE

10 - MAGIC

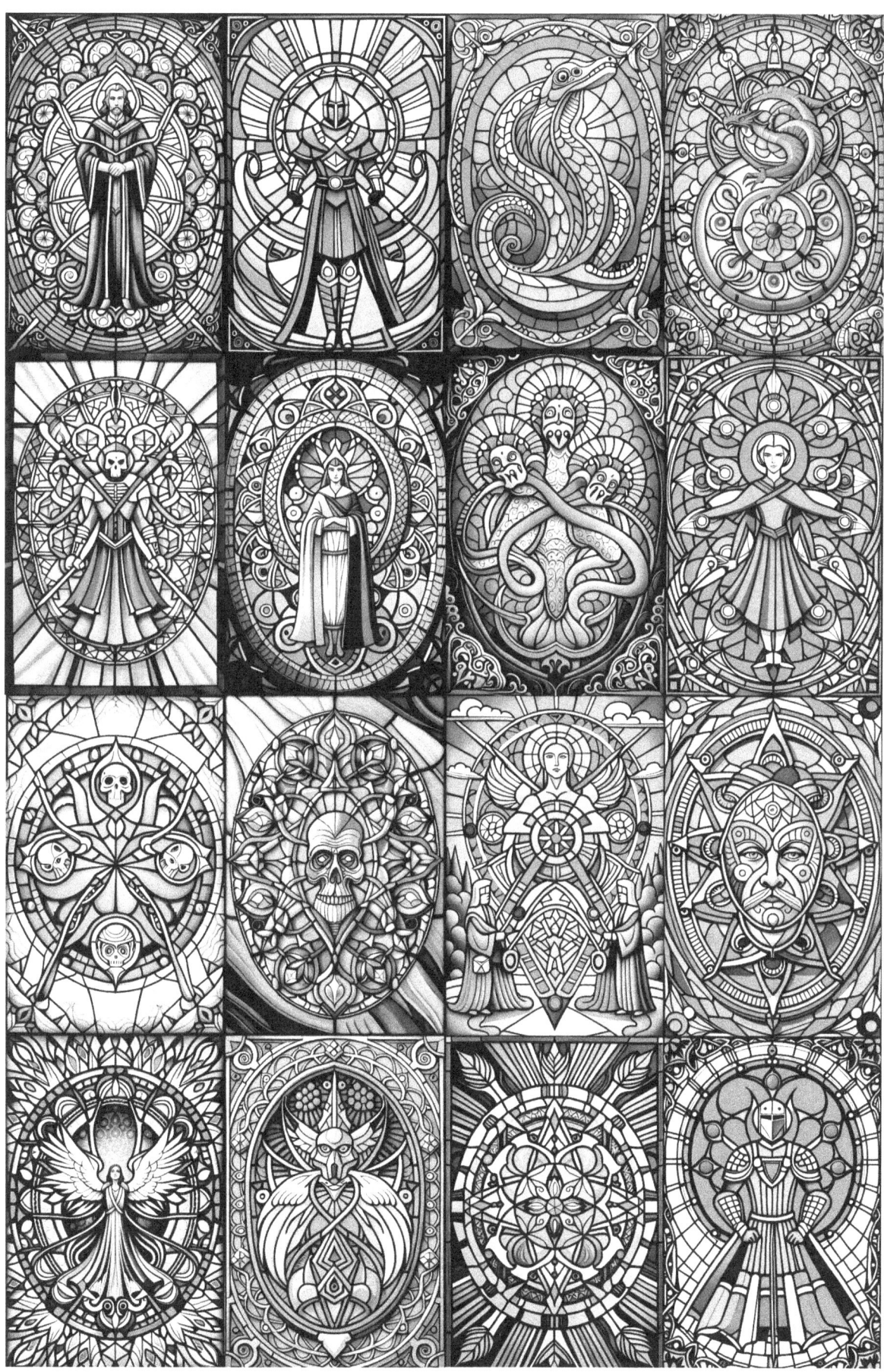

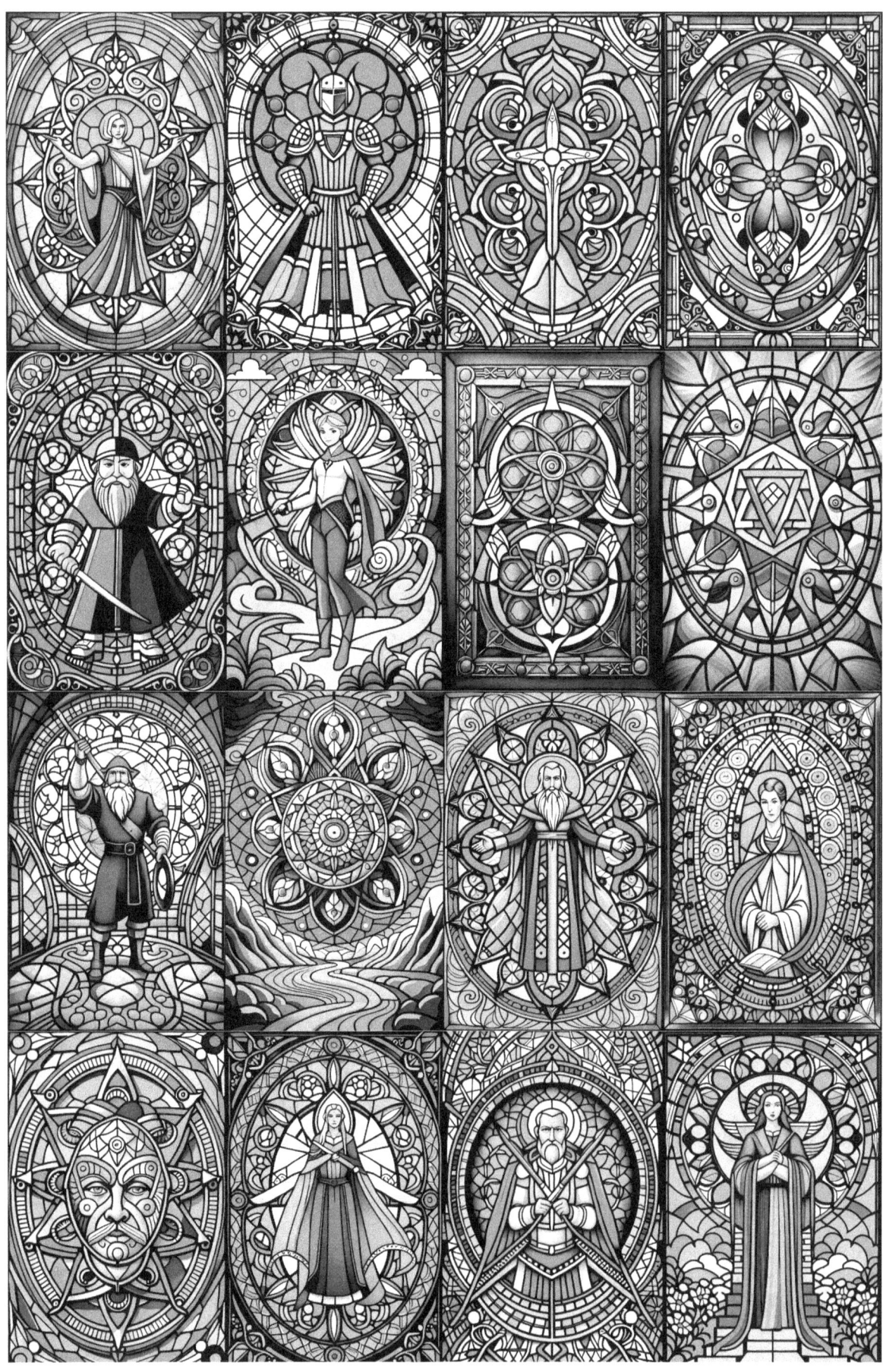

www.ingramcontent.com/pod-product-compliance
Lightning Source LLC
Chambersburg PA
CBHW081456220526
45466CB00008B/2674